How To Make Money Renting A Room In Your Home

How To Make Money Renting A Room In Your Home

THE GUIDE TO FINDING THE RIGHT TENANTS AND MANAGING THE LANDLORD-TENANT RELATIONSHIP

Antonia M. Martin

ISBN-10: 1516933664
ISBN-13: 9781516933662

Library of Congress Control Number: 2015915050
CreateSpace Independent Publishing Platform
North Charleston, South Carolina

Disclaimer
The contents of this publication reflect the view of the author and are an
accumulation of information gathered throughout her experience renting a
room in her home.

This publication is sold with the understanding that the author is not en-
gaged in rendering professional real estate, legal, tax, investment, insurance,
financial, accounting, or other professional advice or services. If the reader requires such advice or services, a competent professional should be consulted.
Relevant laws vary from state to state. The strategies outlined in this book may
not be suitable for every individual, and are not guaranteed or warranted to
produce any particular results.

Although every effort has been made to ensure that the information in this
book was correct at press time, the author and the publisher do not assume
and disclaim any liability to any person or entity for any loss, risk, damage or
disruption caused or alleged to be caused, directly or indirectly, during the
use and application of any of the information contained in this book. The
reader assumes all responsibilities and agrees to hold in no way the author or
the publisher responsible for how s/he utilizes the information.

Any perceived slights of specific persons, peoples or organizations are not
intentional. This book offers practical advice, but makes no guarantees of income made. Readers must use their own judgment regarding their individual
circumstances and values and act in agreement with them.

ACKNOWLEDGEMENTS

I would like to express my appreciation to Melissa Anderson for being my mentor as I started this process and for being so generous in sharing her experiences. I would have climbed a much rockier and steeper path without her help.

I want my editor, Sarah Schroeder, to know how much I appreciate her help in making this a better book.

I'd like to thank my sister, Kelly Martin. She was my sounding board for this project and source of encouragement from beginning to end. I am grateful to Frank Farr for graciously using his newspaperman and English-teacher expertise to proofread my book, and I appreciate his special ability to see the beauty and uniqueness in others.

I'd like to thank my friend, Marty Avary, for taking the time to thoroughly read my early manuscript and make thoughtful suggestions. I'd also like to thank Judi Lebanowski and Brian Rafferty for being early readers.

I'd like to express deep gratitude to my parents, whose perennial belief in me gave me the courage (and sometimes audacity) to take risks and persevere.

Finally, I'd like to thank all of my tenants for teaching me so many valuable lessons.

TABLE OF CONTENTS

PREFACE

Are you looking for a way to make some extra money? Do you know someone who is struggling financially, and you wish you could help?

Have you considered renting a room in your home but are intimidated by the prospect? Have you been renting a room in your home, but would like to make the process smoother and the income more consistent?

This book provides you with a thorough turnkey system for renting a room in your home. It is for people of all ages, all backgrounds, and all education levels who own a home (or have a lease on a home that allows subletting) and want to supplement their income. This book will teach you how and why the process works, how to find compatible tenants, and how to successfully manage the landlord-tenant relationship.

This book is NOT about Airbnb, creating a boarding house with multiple tenants, generating income through nightly or weekly rentals, or becoming a room-renting tycoon.

This comprehensive guide will teach you how to generate reliable income from your home month after month while maintaining your privacy, safety and control of your living environment. This book will flatten the learning curve so you don't have to figure out the process the hard way.

Antonia M. Martin
San Antonio, Texas
October 2015
www.AntoniaMMartin.com

How to Use this Book

I f you are considering renting a room for the first time, start at the beginning of this book. The book provides step-by-step information to build your knowledge and understanding of what you need to know, what you need to do (and what not do), and how to do it. It will teach you how to maintain your privacy, safety and control of your living environment. It will also build your confidence and improve your income.

If you have been renting a room and want to make the process smoother and the income more consistent, you may want to pick chapters selectively and read those sections first. The chapters "Secrets to Attracting High Quality Renters" through "Nuts and Bolts" may give you insights or new ideas.

Regardless of your experience level, it's important to have a strong grasp on the fundamentals for any endeavor. The information in "The Basics" and "The Foundation" should fill in some gaps for you. This book may also help you identify some dynamics and processes you have observed or experienced as a landlord but couldn't quite put your finger on.

Whichever way you choose to read this book, each chapter will give you valuable insights and instructions that will smooth your path to increased income.

INTRODUCTION

This is The Guide to generating income by renting a room in your home. Maintaining your privacy, safety and control of your living environment while making extra money living with a stranger requires coordination and management. It's more complicated than just getting a body into that extra room and cashing a rent check every month. It requires understanding the dynamics and processes that make for a smooth and positive experience for both landlord and tenant.

This guide will provide detailed information about these dynamics and processes, most of which can take years of practical experience to learn and refine. I am sharing knowledge based on seven years of successfully renting a room in my home.

Our homes are the foundation of our lives. If those foundations are peaceful and harmonious, we can reach to greater heights. If they are rocky, inhospitable, hostile, it can be harder to get a handle on the rest of our lives. If mismanaged, the landlord-tenant dynamic will disrupt your life. The purpose of this guide is to teach you how to keep your foundation solid while bringing in reliable extra income.

After reading this guide, another source won't be necessary. It will teach you how to:

- Rapidly develop your skills for the screening and selection process;
- Fill vacancies quicker and easier with the most compatible tenants;
- Create a smoother, more harmonious experience while your tenant is living in your home;
- Reduce stress of the unknown;
- Increase confidence in yourself and your ability to manage this process;
- Flatten the learning curve so you don't have to learn the hard way; and
- Increase your income so you can meet your financial goals.
- Maintain your privacy, safety and control of your living environment.

You would have to read multiple books to acquire the information included in this guide. Internet searches on this topic reveal a variety of short, superficial, conveniently numbered steps, which are often filled with conflicting information. Everything you need to know about successfully navigating this process can be found in these pages.

Who I Am and Why I Rent a Room

I am a single business woman in my 50's who loves the outdoors. Like many others during the tough times of the recent years, I felt the financial pinch. I was lucky to have a friend who had successfully rented rooms in her home, and her experience intrigued me. I had an extra room, so I thought about renting it out too. However, I wasn't sure it was the right thing for me. I was intimidated by the prospect of letting a stranger live in my home and by the thought of figuring out, starting and managing the process.

One obstacle for me was my previous experiences with room-mates, which I did not want to repeat. I didn't want to share my home and personal space with someone who wouldn't value my home as much as I did. I dreaded the thought of dealing with the inevitable differences in our values and personalities, differing attitudes and behaviors towards cleanliness and privacy, and the challenge of negotiating shared bills. I had worked hard to own my own home and be in charge of my own space. I didn't want to share the rights and privileges of home ownership with a stranger who hadn't earned them.

Over the last seven years, with some advice from my friend and plenty of trial and error, I developed a successful system for renting a room. I know the system is generally applicable, because I have shared it with others, and it has worked for them too. Over the years, the extra money has ranged from being a nice budget addition to saving my financial skin.

After discussing this topic with many people, I realized that my concerns and experience renting a room were typical, and that I could help other people who might be interested in earning some extra money. I have taught my system to others, and it has worked well for them too.

Why Did I Write This?
When I first considered renting a room, I was intimidated by how much I needed to learn, and I wanted to make sure I got it right. I knew that a slow learning curve with mistakes could be costly and might also make my life uncomfortable. After discussing this

topic with many people, I realized that these same issues intimidate most people who consider renting a room.

To ease the learning curve and reduce my mistakes, I talked to my friend who'd done it successfully before. She was very helpful, and she walked me through her process. She shared some of the documents she used, which I adapted for my own use. She provided a starting point, which saved me a lot of time and reduced some of the trial and error. I felt encouraged, like this was something I could actually do. She was a good friend, and I will always be grateful for her help. I know how valuable a hand up can be in this process, and that's why I'm writing this book: to pass along the hand up and simplify an intimidating and intricate process.

Because I'm an analytical person, I like to figure out systems for doing just about anything. When some of my friends noticed that this room-renting-thing was working well, they began asking my advice. When I shared my system, my friends found the process easier and less intimidating than they had imagined. Sharing my system made me realize I had inadvertently created a thorough turnkey system with valuable insights for people interested in making money renting a room in their home.

So here is the system that has worked well for me and my friends. This book provides the information needed to make an informed decision about renting a room in your home. This book will help you answer three important questions:

- Is this what you want to do?
- Will it work for you?
- How do you do it?

This book provides all the information you will need to be successful, while only treading lightly upon the learning curve. In the University of Life, it is easier to learn from the mistakes and experience of others. Learn from mine.

CHAPTER 1

THE BASICS

What's the Difference between Renting a Room and Having a Roommate?

Control. It's Your House, Your Rules

It's important to understand the difference between a roommate and a room renter. Understanding the differences between having a roommate and renting a room requires exploring the dynamics of both.

Roommate

- The entire house is shared, usually equally.
- Roommates have their personal possessions that must be accommodated (furniture, kitchen items, decorations, etc.).
- Roommates must cope with differences in personality and living habits (cleanliness vs. messiness, social vs. private, loud vs. quiet, considerate vs. inconsiderate, etc.).
- Roommates' friends, guests, boy/girlfriends, family members and all the drama surrounding those relationships must be contended with.

- Responsibilities around the house and yard must be shared and managed. Sharing household responsibilities is always a challenge, and a roommate is never going to be as committed to your home as you are.
- Roommates' lives intertwine, so it becomes a personal relationship. The daily ins and outs of a roommate's life, and their impact on your life, are ever present and inescapable.
- You do not have much control over your living situation.
- Boundaries between roommates tend to blur.
- It can be complicated to extricate yourself if things don't work out.
- Bills are shared (usually split by some percentage). The task of getting money out of a roommate every month can be challenging.
- Roommates share part of the housing payment and part of the bills.

Room Renter

- Room renters pay for only a bedroom and bathroom, and possibly other specific areas, with optional privileges for using the kitchen, dining room and laundry room. (More on privileges in "What Do You Have to Offer the Tenant" in Chapter 2.)
- Room renters have few possessions that you don't have to rearrange your house to accommodate. (More on this in "The Nature of Room Renters" in Chapter 2.)
- You have most of the house to yourself. A majority of the house is still your domain.
- You are responsible for most, if not all, of the housework and yard work. The room renter will be responsible for taking

care of his bedroom, maybe his bathroom, and is expected to clean up after himself after using any "privilege" areas.

- Relationships with room renters range from personal to impersonal. There's very little drama, if any, because you seldom see him. The renter stays in the part of the house he's renting, and only occasionally ventures into other areas of the house for which he has privileges, like the kitchen and laundry room. He doesn't hang out in those "privilege" areas; he uses them briefly as needed and then returns to his room.

- Clear, firm boundaries are established from the beginning. You have control over your environment. You are the one taking the risk and managing the responsibilities of home ownership. You call the shots.

- It's relatively simple to extricate yourself if things don't work out.

- The room renter pays one fee each month. Bills are included in the rent.

Benefits of Renting a Room

The most important benefit of renting a room is that it is great to have the extra money; it can save you financially. Renting a room can provide the extra money to pay off bills, buy something special, update the house, take a trip, go back to school, maintain your preferred lifestyle, or fulfill any just-out-of-reach dream. Financial studies have shown that just $400 or $500 a month can make the difference between financial disaster and pulling through tough times. I know it did for me.

Remember when you were younger and lived with your parents? They probably said, "It's my house: my rules. Someday, when you get a place of your own, you can make the rules. Until then, you follow my rules." Well, now you have your own place. So make it your rules.

The room renter relationship is more like a business relationship. Since it's your house, you're in the driver's seat. If you don't like the room renter, you can ask him to leave. You're not at the mercy of a delicate roommate situation where your lives are more entangled personally and financially.

You don't live alone, yet you're not crowded: the room renter is living in your home with limited access to it. To my surprise, I found it reassuring to have someone else around.

If you have to leave home for travel, someone is there to watch over the place. At one point I had a job where I traveled two long days a week to the Mexican border and the gulf coast. It was reassuring to know there was someone at home to keep my cats company or in case something happened. On one occasion when I was away on a week's vacation, an intense storm hit. Part of my neighbor's tree cracked and fell into my yard. When my tenant called to notify me, we were able to strategize, and the problem was resolved by the time I got home. Having someone in residence while you're away from home can be a stabilizing factor.

Understand the Value of What You Are Offering

You need to understand what renting a room means, and what benefits you're offering a prospective tenant so you can:

- Position yourself competitively in the room-renting-market
- Set workable limits
- Set appropriate expectations for you and the tenant

Once I understood and adjusted to the dynamics of renting a room, my experience vastly improved (along with my finances).

Finances for the tenant are compact. All bills are included. Tenants only have to manage one payment for all living expenses: it is not rent *plus* utilities, *plus* internet, *plus* water, *plus* garbage, *plus* cable, *plus* land line. Renting a room is more economical for room renters. They pay far less than they would in a roommate situation.

Most people seeking a room to rent are looking for ways to save money. You are providing them a way to meet financial goals while they are helping you to meet yours.

Tenants have access to a fully equipped kitchen. You provide pots, pans, utensils, plates, bowls, cutlery, glasses, etc. They bring along very little, if anything. They walk into a kitchen that's ready to use with no effort or contribution on their part.

Allowing access to laundry facilities at your home means that tenants don't have to fuss with the inconvenience, time constraints and security issues of using a Laundromat. In seven years, my tenants have only washed a couple of loads every two or three weeks, that's it. Allowing use of laundry facilities is very valuable to tenants, and it has minimal impact on your life.

If you chose to allow dining room privileges, tenants will have the home-like atmosphere of eating at a table rather than always eating in their room. In my experience, allowing dining room privileges has been perceived as an added bonus but was rarely used, thereby offering an enhancement without having to actually give up more space in my home.

If you allow access to other parts of your home, it makes the tenant's living situation more home-like and more attractive.

This can make you more competitive in attracting higher quality renters. I allow use of an extra bedroom that I turned into a study/library as part of the room rental. In three years, the tenants have rarely used it. Prospective tenants perceive use of that extra room as a benefit, yet I haven't had to deal with them using it when I wanted to.

The room renter just shows up and has the use of a home without the responsibilities of one. He doesn't have to own or schlep personal belongings like furniture, kitchen items, decorations, or other household necessities. He isn't expected to share in household duties like housework and yard work (except to clean up his own messes, of course). He doesn't have to pay extra bills. He doesn't have to contend with contrary living habits of fellow apartment dwellers. He gets to live in a home-like setting with very little effort. It's an incredibly convenient arrangement for the room renter.

You provide the room renter with a living situation with plenty of privacy and simplicity. There should be no drama, no uncomfortable roommate interactions, and no worries.

The landlord is a person he knows, not a faceless management company or absentee landlord. The room rental arrangement is more personal than renting a house or apartment, yet at the same time is less personal than having a roommate. It's a handy hybrid.

CHAPTER 2

THE FOUNDATION

The Nature of Room Renters

The nature of a room renter is different from someone who is looking for a roommate or wanting to rent an apartment or house. Once I figured out the nature of a room renter, I was able to shift gears in a way that increased my success. I altered my approach, adjusted my marketing, attracted higher quality prospects and was more satisfied with the process. It's important to understand a room renter's nature so you can set appropriate expectations for them, yourself and this endeavor.

Often room renters are transitory people. They tend to fall into several categories.

The Scouts

These are people moving into town, looking for a place to live and getting the lay of the land before selecting a permanent location. Sometimes they are single, and sometimes they are spouses coming into town first. This prospective renter will be looking for a room for about one to three months. You'll need to ascertain the minimum length of time you'll require a renter to stay. By setting a minimum time requirement for residency, you will set appropriate expectations and screen out prospective renters that don't meet your requirements.

Frequently, this type of renter is a professional and will possess organizational skills and follow through that the average type of room renter won't possess. This will enable the two of you to make arrangements over a geographic distance. You may not meet this person before he moves in. Occasionally he may make a quick weekend recon trip and squeeze you into a busy exploratory schedule. This type of renter will frequently want you to hold the room for him. Only hold a room when you've got money in hand.

Since you know this type of room renter is guaranteed to be short term, it can be a little easier to take a chance with them. If they don't work out, you aren't stuck with them for long. Keep in mind that not knowing or meeting you before moving in can be risky for them as well. They don't know what they're getting into either.

On one occasion I made arrangements with a room renter from out of state. He was starting employment at a nearby employer, and he was the scout for his family. We emailed back and forth, talked on the phone and made all arrangements via telephone and email. I required a money order for the deposit and first month's rent plus all paperwork signed before I would cease my tenant search. When I picked him up at the airport, it was the first time we met. It was a *calculated* risk for both of us, and it worked out well.

Passing through Town

Other room renters will be passing through town for a variety of reasons, mostly due to work. They plan to live in town for a matter of months and are looking for a living situation that is better than living in a motel. This type of tenant has an expiration date printed on him.

Ending a Relationship

Another type of room renter is one who is just getting out of a relationship. He needs a simple, uncomplicated interim living situation without strings or long-term commitments. His tenancy can vary widely. This type of tenant may seem a bit prone to drama and instability, but it isn't necessarily true. In the preliminary phone conversation and initial meeting, you can gauge his "drama level."

One of my "ending-relationship" tenants was separating and getting a divorce from his wife. When I interviewed him I got the sense there was no drama and he was basically a stable guy. My home was the first home in several decades he'd lived in that wasn't his own. He had a teenage son that he visited regularly and occasionally brought over. He wasn't around much and I rarely saw or spoke to him. He barely used the house and never used the kitchen; he mostly just used the house as a place to sleep. When he moved out three months later, he moved into a home he purchased.

Diplomatically ask these types of prospects enough questions to make you feel comfortable with their emotional and psychological frame of mind. They expect you to ask these questions.

These types of tenants can be wishy-washy about whether they're going to move in or not. Don't waste too much time or energy chasing them. Frequently they don't know if they're really moving, when they need to move or where they're going to go. While they may not be unstable, their life situation is. Making decisions or commitments is always problematic during this phase of life.

At one point I was going through a dry spell trying to find tenants, and I emailed and talked with the no-drama tenant I previously mentioned. He came for a visit; it seemed to go well, and he expressed his intent to move in. Then I didn't hear from him. Suddenly after three weeks of no contact, he emailed that he wanted to move in immediately. This is how it can go with the "relationship-ending" room renter. Firmly set expectations up front, pay particular attention to the paperwork and do not get involved with their story.

College Students

Another common tenant source is college students. They are a mixed bag. They are still learning about the world and how it works, and they are exploring their limits and those of others. Consequently they tend to be unreliable. They also tend to be the most compliant with house rules and can be a longer-term tenant.

Students are focused on goals, may be working a job in addition to school and tend to be more respectful of your home. Most have recently left a family environment and don't want or know how to care for a place of their own. Most students haven't yet accumulated the possessions necessary for a home. All this makes renting a room in a private home ideal for them.

Students will tend to be busy and the little time they are around will usually be spent in their rooms studying or sleeping. Of course with college students, some will be partiers. If you don't want a partier, it's easy enough to screen them out in the ad you place and during the preliminary phone call and face-to-face interview.

The Retired Person

Another type of room renter is the retired person. This is my favorite. He doesn't want responsibilities and is the most mature type of tenant. He keeps to himself, is quiet and little trouble. This type tends to appreciate a quiet, peaceful home over a social, busy one.

The Mess

Then there's the mess. This one is easy to spot: Mama calls.

If Mama is calling, her son is most likely immature, lacking in life skills and not capable of calling for himself. Perhaps he won't leave the nest. Or he's living in a situation Mama doesn't approve of.

This type of tenant will not follow rules and will not do what he says he will do. His understanding of social rules and responsibility level will be low. His room and bathroom will be a disaster area. Let your unwise competition have him.

Reliability Isn't Their Strong Suit

On average, most room renters are going to be unreliable to some degree (some more than others). Even normally reliable, dependable people will be less so when they know their residency will be short. Room renters don't want the responsibilities of their own place. Most don't possess the skills to manage a home. If they did, they'd be renting an apartment or house or looking for a roommate situation. They aren't interested in taking care of a home, doing housework or yard work. They are looking for a simple living environment.

Don't expect reliability and dependability from room renters; that's why completing the paperwork and upholding it is so important. Room renters have a tendency to *not* follow through with what they say they're going to do. Expecting otherwise can create frustration.

When I first started renting a room, I required a small amount of housework and yard work as part of my package. I was blending elements of a roommate situation into this new-to-me room renter arrangement. I had two experiences with it. Most prospective tenants ran. They wanted nothing to do with responsibilities around the house. Tenants that signed on didn't do the work despite agreeing to it. They resented being reminded to do it. I resented reminding them to do it. It was a recipe for frustration for both of us.

Now I only require tenants to promptly clean up after themselves when using the "privilege" areas of the house. I gave up expecting them to keep the bathroom in presentable condition. I increased the rent by $25 and keep the bathroom clean myself. This has continued to work well and prospective tenants are comfortable with these expectations. When pricing your room, you will be wise to factor in the costs of keeping up the house and yard on your own.

Private People

Room renters tend to be private and keep to themselves. They like their own space and tend to stay in their rooms. Even though use of the dining room, a library/study and a nice screened-in porch are available for their use, my tenants have rarely used them. Offering use of these parts of the house is considered a plus to prospective tenants, yet I am able to keep most of the house to myself.

Male Preponderance

All but one of my tenants has been male. You'll find a vast majority of room-renter prospects are male. I personally think this is because most women are nesters. They want a home of their own, and many women possess the skills to make a home. Women also may want a more social or communal living situation than renting a room offers.

All of the male room renters have made their room into a man cave. They usually keep it dark and watch TV, spend time on the computer and/or play video games (and study if a student). Renting a room is an ideal situation for many males. They do not have to communicate, participate in social interactions, perform household duties or do anything other than watch TV or work/study/play on the computer.

Renters Who Are or Have Been Homeowners

The Scout, Passing-Through-Town, Relationship-Ending and Retiree tenants are frequently homeowners or former homeowners. In the early days of renting a room, I was particularly surprised by my inappropriate expectations for homeowners.

It's curious how expectations can be so wrong. I thought home-owners would be the most respectful of my home; I thought they would appreciate the need to take care of one's living space.

On the contrary, I found their bathrooms were the dirtiest, they left the worst messes to clean up after moving out, and a homeowner was the only tenant that ever damaged my home. Consistently and without exception, homeowners were the most disrespectful of my home. It's probably because they are used to calling the shots in their own homes and aren't used to (and don't like) following someone else's rules.

Because I expected the homeowners to understand respect-ful treatment of a home, I didn't emphasize the paperwork or house rules when they moved in. From these tenants, I learned the importance of thoroughly reviewing the paperwork and house rules when a tenant moves in and continuously upholding those rules. Luckily, they were short-term tenants.

A Few Last Words Regarding the Nature of Room Renters

Putting down and maintaining roots require certain skills, traits and values that many room renters don't possess. Some room renters might possess them, but they are in transition and those life skills, responsible traits and personal values may be on holi-day while living with you. Since you have your own home, you obviously possess the required skills, traits and values. If you keep in mind that room renters will tend to be very different from you, you'll set appropriate expectations for them, the process and the enterprise.

Short-Term Versus Long-Term Tenants

It's important to understand the nature of short-term and long-term tenants. It will help you decide if you want one over the other, or if it matters. When I understood the dynamics of both, I was able to market better to prospective tenants and to set expectations for the tenants and myself.

Short-Term Tenants

This type of tenant might be the safest and easiest tenant to start with because he is in your home for a short period of time. Being short term can make it easier to tolerate annoyances: they won't be staying long. If you make a mistake in choosing the person or how the arrangement is set up, he'll be moving on and you can make a fresh start with the next tenant. It's less risk.

Short-term tenants require you to perform the tenant search, orient tenants to the household rules and adjust to their particular ways more frequently. Until you develop proficiency in finding renters, there will be more risk of vacancy and income loss in between each tenant. After you figure out the process, there will be less vacancy. The room will be filled quicker and easier with tenants that are more compatible. The lessons you learn from this book will substantially reduce the dry spells.

Long-Term Tenants

With a compatible fit, there is more stability. There are fewer breaks in income due to vacancies. Longer-term tenants get used to your household rules and become more comfortable with them. They tend to grow more attached to your home as their home and you may grow more attached to them.

With long-term tenants, you have to live with the annoyances longer, and over time you will have more exposure to them. It's especially important that you set up the living arrangement properly from the initial move-in meeting and continue to reinforce house rules. If reinforcement slips, it's hard to rein it back in and much easier to keep letting other important areas slip. The more rules the tenant encroaches upon, the less satisfied you will be with the experience.

With one of my longer-term tenants, I set up an agreement that he keep his bathroom clean and mop the kitchen floor every other week. After a few months, he "forgot" to do these things. It would have been easier in the short term if I did not bother with reminding him. But in the long term, my annoyance would have grown into resentment.

Since we didn't see each other very often, I left notes in his bathroom stating that it needed to be cleaned, or that the kitchen floor needed to be mopped. If it didn't get done within a few days, I made a point to talk briefly to him about it. I created a habit over time of *not* letting these important issues slide. As a result, the tenants have learned not to push other rules as much or as often. They know I hold my line. Holding the line with longer-term tenants will create a more pleasant experience.

Common Concerns

When I discuss renting a room with people, their concerns consistently fall within a few categories about the risks. There are risks involved. The more you know, the less apprehensive you'll be and the better you can design your processes and living situation to substantially reduce or avoid the risks.

Security and Safety

You *are* letting someone you don't know (or don't know well) into your home. This person will have access to your personal life and property. That is a risk.

The risk can be reduced with background and credit checks. You can learn a lot about people from their credit reports. The information from background checks and/or credit reports can help ease your mind if this is a big concern for you.

I've gotten to the point that I don't pull background checks or credit reports anymore. I tell prospects I am going to and ask them if there is anything they want to tell me about before I do. One of four things happens:

1. They immediately excuse themselves from consideration.
2. They tell me it's okay and then contact me later to tell me they're no longer interested.
3. They tell me about issues I would have found.
4. They have no worries because there's nothing to find.

I can acquire a good sense of a person through the screening process I've developed. The initial interview aspect of the screening process is a crucial step in getting a sense of the person. We all have gut instincts and intuition that can be an important screening tool. Sometimes a person just "feels off" in the preliminary phone conversation or at the interview. It's nothing substantial, it's a sense you get, and it is important to listen to those instincts.

I don't recommend pulling or not pulling background checks and/or credit reports. You may never pull them, like my friend who initially mentored me. You may want to pull them at first and eventually find you don't need them. Or you may pull them on every serious prospective tenant. You'll find what feels most comfortable for you. (Regardless of what you choose, the screening process described in this book will play an important role in selecting tenants.)

Fear Someone Is Casing the Joint

Occasionally someone will bring up this concern. They are concerned that individuals coming to their home are going to inspect it for prospective breaking and entering opportunities. If this is one of your concerns, there are processes to help address it.

The most important thing you can do to avoid being cased is *do not* skip the telephone conversation aspect of the screening process. Talk with the prospects long enough to get a feel for them. You can tell them, as a security precaution and for your feelings of safety, that you require a picture ID for all prospective tenants coming to your home. This will indicate to visitors you are paying attention and those with ulterior motives will be put off.

Don't write down driver's license numbers at the interview. If someone gets a hold of that identity-sensitive information and misuses it, you are liable both civilly and criminally for its misuse. *At this point*, don't go so far as taking down their driver's license numbers due to the potential liability, and because most reasonable people will not want you, a stranger, to have it yet for the same reasons.

How Will Renting a Room Affect My Homeowner's Insurance?

That's a good question. You will be generating income from an additional person living in your home. Will that make your insurance go up? Will it nullify your insurance policy? Should you just not say anything – don't ask, don't tell?

I called a variety of insurance companies, both large and small, when I was looking for a homeowner's insurance policy. I asked each company how renting a room in my home would affect my coverage. For most insurance companies, having a room renter had no effect on my policy, as long as I continued to live in my home.

Insurance companies set a limit on how many room renters you can have without changing the policy or increasing the premium. Some set the limit at one person; some set it at two. When the limit was exceeded, some companies changed the type of policy, and other companies increased the premium.

Some insurance companies will cover rental income loss when there is a written lease in place if the house becomes uninhabitable due to a covered catastrophe, such as a fire. All the insurance companies recommended that the tenant purchase his own renter's insurance, because the tenant's personal property is not covered under the landlord's policy.

Of course, you need to do your own research for your home and your state. Here are some questions to ask:

1. Will your homeowner's insurance policy or premium be affected if you rent a room in your home to a tenant while you're still living there?
2. Is there a limit to how many tenants you can have without affecting your policy or premium?

3. If your home becomes uninhabitable due to a covered catastrophe, will the policy cover loss of rental income?
4. Does your policy cover the tenant's personal property?

Wear and Tear Caused by That Extra Person

Another common concern is the issue of extra wear and tear on the house from an added resident. This was also one of my important concerns. But in reality, because of the way I've set up the room renting arrangement, wear and tear hasn't been an issue.

For one thing, use and access to the house is limited. Remember, this is *not* a roommate situation where the house is shared equally and the entire house is subject to another person's habits and life style, which translates into wear and tear. The room renter is not going to use that much of the house.

With the room renting system, you set firm ground rules. Unlike a roommate arrangement, the tenant doesn't get to do whatever he wants. You have set the ground rules, and he's agreed to abide by them. If you require a deposit and require the tenant to clean up after himself, the tenant will have more respect for your home, which ultimately results in less wear and tear.

It's important to keep an eye on how the tenant is treating your house. Don't let any behavior go too far. If a tenant is pushing the edge of the rules, calmly but firmly remind him of the agreements. Don't let things slide.

You know the saying, "Money Talks?" If you require a large enough deposit, the tenant's money will whisper to him, reminding him to be responsible. Since I learned to require a deposit large enough that it would hurt if forfeited, tenants have maintained their responsibilities, and I have fewer messes to clean up after they leave.

The Bills Will Cost More

Many people have voiced this concern. It was another one of mine. However, I found (to my surprise) the household energy and water usage showed a minimal increase with a tenant.

Tenant showers and laundry barely add to the water bill. I noticed no difference between when I have a tenant and when I don't. When it comes to energy usage, the house has to be heated and cooled anyway; one extra body doesn't make much difference. The tenant's extra energy usage from lights and electronics, barely makes a difference in the total utility bill.

Afraid the Changes Required Will Be Too Difficult or Uncomfortable

Come on, you're not made of china; you're not going to break. At first it may be a bit uncomfortable because you're used to things a certain way and you have to do some rearranging. You may have to clean out that room and rearrange things in your home a bit. You'll need to make room in the refrigerator and pantry for their food. Most renters won't use it or will actually use very little space. It's the nature of room renters.

After a while the new way will grow familiar. You may need to loosen up a bit. Remember, you're still going to have most of the house to yourself. You just can't run around naked or in your skivvies anymore, or at least not when the tenant is around. In Texas we have a saying, "Get your big boy pants on." You can handle it. The extra income will be worth it.

Loss of Privacy

Like most people renting a room in their house, I didn't like the idea of losing my privacy. But once again, I found my apprehension was unfounded. Loss of privacy hasn't been a problem.

The tenant is occupying a part of the house that likely is not getting used anyway or is used very little, except perhaps for storage. Room renters tend to stick to themselves. You retain control over the rest of the house.

What if I Don't Like Them?

Having someone in your home that you don't like is an unpleasant prospect. It might happen, especially in the beginning before you develop skill from the screening system. For the most part, inappropriate tenants will be screened out with the system described in this book.

If you are highly concerned, consider short-term tenants, at least until you have developed your process to a comfortable level. I had a few short-term tenants I didn't care for, but I knew they weren't going to be around for long. It made it easier to tolerate the things that annoyed me about them.

Remember, this isn't a roommate situation. It's your house, your rules. If you really don't like a tenant, ask him to leave.

I have only asked one tenant to leave. I knew in the beginning we weren't compatible.

I was still new to the process of renting a room in my home and wasn't good at it yet. I was making a lot of mistakes which this book is geared to prevent. I was scaring off prospective tenants which resulted in a six-week vacancy. I hadn't figured out what type of tenant was a good fit so my ads were drawing a lot of inappropriate prospects. I was being overly strict in my requirements, acted with little confidence in the face-to-face interview, and my expectations were inappropriate for room renters.

When this incompatible tenant agreed to move in, I knew it wasn't going to work. I went against my instincts and the result was predictable. Follow your instincts, follow this system and you'll be unlikely to have this experience.

Concerns about renting a room in your home are legitimate. To ascertain if it's worth learning a new set of behaviors ask yourself two questions. How willing are you to stretch, learn new things and grow? How much do you need or want the extra money?

Everyone has different needs and tolerance levels. Once you've rented a room for a while, you'll develop a unique system that meets your needs and works best for you. As experience grows, so will your comfort level. It's the nature of life. The more you do something, the better you'll get at it and the more comfortable it will feel.

It's important not to focus too much on your concerns or imagined potential problems. Problems are always worse in anticipation than in reality. There are important benefits to renting a room, so focus on them as well. The more you know about the enterprise you're considering, the less you're going to learn the hard way, thereby accelerating to a positive experience and increasing your income.

Analyze Your Situation

It's important to analyze your situation on a variety of levels. What are your needs? What do you want in a tenant? What do you have to offer? How much of your living space do you want to share?

Doing this analysis makes the process less intimidating. You will use this analysis as the foundation for designing your room rental and developing your system for marketing, screening and selecting compatible tenants. Analysis will save time, energy and money as well as lead to better, more compatible choices. It won't necessarily be something done all at one time, though it could be. Most likely it will be something that gestates over time.

What Are Your Needs?

Do you need more money? If so, what do you need it for? How precarious is your financial situation? Would it be nice to have the money? Will the money save your financial butt? Or are you somewhere in between?

At first I started renting a room because I was feeling the vise of the troubled financial times, and needed the extra money to survive. Once I got on my feet, I kept renting a room. I realized that it was nice having the extra money. I also didn't want to lose the momentum of renting a room. I didn't want to get rusty at the process. By continually renting a room, it was easier to keep that momentum moving and keep my hand in the game.

This philosophy served me well when suddenly one of my employers closed its doors, missed the entire last month of payroll and I found myself unexpectedly unemployed for several months. You never know what life is going to throw at you;

renting a room can be a key component in turning lemons into lemonade.

Will you like having a little extra company around? Do you mind living with people? Do you dread the idea of having someone else in your space?

I had really enjoyed living alone and having my home to myself. At first I dreaded bringing someone new into my living space. So it came as a surprise when I found that I actually liked having someone else around. It's nice having my place to myself when there's a brief vacancy. Then I'm relieved to have someone back in the house when I find a new tenant. Renting a room provides the best of both worlds. You have someone around, but you don't have to interact with them much.

How important is your privacy? Are you a very private individual, a social butterfly or somewhere in between? Where you fall on this spectrum will help you determine how to set up your living arrangement. Since it's your house, your rules, you get to design the living arrangement to meet your privacy or social needs.

What Do You Want in a Tenant?
You have to figure out what you want and don't want in a tenant in order to be successful in this endeavor. Use this information as a guide when designing the living arrangement, marketing for and selecting a tenant. It will lead to better choices and better experiences.

The best way to identify what you want in a tenant is to create a list. Making a list will help you clarify your focus. Be clear about what you want, because you will use this as a guide when writing the tenant ads. If you outline what you are looking for, the screening process will be more efficient, and you can be more effective when communicating through email, phone and face-to-face interviews. You will find more compatible people, and you will have a more positive, lucrative experience because you were clear about what you wanted.

To illustrate my point, I'll share with you my original list:

- Gone most of the time
- Quiet
- No guests
- Female, non-smoker, non-student, non-drinker, non-drug user
- Animal lover
- Doesn't watch TV
- Doesn't cook
- Mentally healthy
- Doesn't have much stuff
- Only washes a few loads of laundry every other week

That was my *original* list. It has evolved over time and is still evolving. I learned that some traits weren't as disagreeable as I thought they would be and that others were important that I hadn't considered. Here is my current list:

- Quiet
- Can have guests as long as they don't become an unofficial second tenant
- Non-smoker and non-drug user
- Easy on the drinking and partying
- At least tolerates animals

- Mentally healthy
- Doesn't have much stuff
- Has a respectful attitude toward me and my home
- No day sleepers

As you learn and grow through experience, your list will also evolve. You'll be exposed to a variety of personalities. You will add and remove desired and undesired characteristics, traits and behaviors on your list, just as I have on mine.

Tenant Characteristics

There are a variety of characteristics to consider that will pop up in prospective tenants. It's best if you anticipate a few of these characteristics in advance to give your search focus. I will cover a few of the important ones to consider.

Day Sleepers

Day sleepers will respond to your ad. These people work at night and need peace and quiet during the day. They will come and go at hours very different from a person with a more conventional schedule. Can you accommodate the needs of a day sleeper, such as being quiet during the day? Will your lifestyle fit with the hours of a day sleeper?

The only time my energy usage increased with a tenant was the one time I had a day sleeper. Tenants with conventional hours won't be using energy during the hours most people sleep. However, with a day sleeper, energy usage is around the clock. You will use it during the day, and a day sleeper will use it during the night.

Social Tenants

Will you be comfortable with a social tenant who brings friends over and has a variety of people coming through your home? Will a partier-type who comes home at all hours, in varying states of sobriety fit your style? Will you allow "sleep-overs?" Would you prefer a quiet tenant who keeps to himself?

Smokers

Will you allow smokers? If so, will you have a designated smoking area for them? Where will it be? How will you expect them to handle their cigarette butts?

I am and always have been a non-smoker. At first I thought I could be open-minded about smoking. I thought it would be alright to allow a smoking tenant as long as he smoked outside and didn't leave cigarette butts around. But what I learned is that, in close quarters, smokers, no matter how diligent they are, will still smell like smoke. It clings to their clothes and exudes from their pores, so their room smells smoky even though they never smoke in it.

From Different Cultures

A number of respondents will be people from other countries and cultures. Renting a room is perfect for these folks. They have different orientations towards cleanliness, morality, communication styles, noise levels, social mores, women, and many other aspects of life. Their English fluency may range somewhere between challenged to excellent. If they cook, they may cook with foods and spices that will create aromas or odors you aren't used to. How open minded and tolerant are you? If you're a woman or have women in your household, can you afford to rent to a person from a culture that may have an inherent disrespect for women?

Short-Term or Long-Term

Another important trait to consider is the term of a tenant. Earlier in Chapter 2 – The Foundation, I described the characteristics of short-term and long-term tenants. Review the descriptions and consider how their characteristics will fit for you.

At first I aimed for long-term tenants, because I thought it would be easier. What I found was that most long-term tenants didn't stay as long as they originally intended. Room renters tend to be a bit flakey, and their lives are less stable than mine. A variety of things would come up in their lives and they moved on within three to six months anyway.

By focusing on long-term tenants, I actually narrowed my options. When I opened up my options to include short-term tenants, I was able to find better quality tenants. I went through more tenants, but I also developed experience and skill at the screening and selection process at a faster rate. I was able to fill vacancies quicker, easier and with more compatible tenants. My confidence grew and prospective tenants responded to that confidence. As a result of my improved skills, I found longer-term, more compatible tenants.

Other Considerations

Does it matter if the person cooks a lot or not all? Do you care if he keeps the bathroom clean or cleans up after himself? Does he need to be an animal lover or at least animal neutral?

These are some common characteristics and traits that you will encounter, so you should consider them in advance. As you communicate with prospective tenants, you'll encounter traits and characteristics you hadn't imagined. Make your list and allow it to evolve.

What Do You Have to Offer a Tenant?

Take stock of your home. Look at it from a renter's perspective. If you were a prospective renter looking at a room in your home, what would you think of the space? It's important to develop a sense of what you have to offer so you know how to price, market and show your home to a tenant. Prospective tenants will be touring other homes. They will be familiar with what else is out there in the market. It's important to understand how you measure up against the competition.

It is also important to read through the ads on Craigslist (www.craigslist.com) under Housing/Rooms & Shares. Investigate what other landlords are offering and what they are charging. Note the amenities they are touting. Get an idea of how your offering measures up against the competition, and consider what things you may want to improve.

Following are specific aspects to analyze about your home and what you have to offer a tenant.

Location, Location, Location

Identify popular places that are close to your home. Get out a map and analyze your area. Look at it like a stranger. Observe the positive and negative aspects of your location. Are you close (say within a 20 minute drive) to: universities, major employers, downtown, points of interest, parks, military bases, historical sites, theme parks, major shopping malls, particularly attractive or prestigious areas? Are you far away from areas that may be considered unpleasant aspects of your area, or are you far away from conveniences?

For example, my home is ideally located within a 15-minute drive to a major university, the largest employer in San Antonio, the major medical center, four large parks, a theme park, the most prestigious subdivision, and a major shopping mall. It's far away from the military bases, downtown or historical sites. How would you analyze your location? This is important to consider when pricing and marketing your room rental.

Easy Access
Is it easy to get to shops, restaurants, grocery stores, gyms, gas stations, parks, strip malls, post office, bus stops, major highways or roads for easy commuting? Is it awkward or inconvenient to access these amenities? You don't need to make negative or discouraging judgments; you just need to take note right now.

Furnished Versus Unfurnished
Do you have an empty, unfurnished bedroom? Will the tenant need to bring his own furniture? Will the rented room have a bed, dresser, table, desk, chair, sofa, ceiling fan, adequate lighting, art on the walls, and/or curtains on the windows? Will it be a homey room or a sparse one?

The first time I rented a room, it was empty, with no furnishings. I quickly learned through experience that most room renters were looking for at least some furniture, especially a quality bed with linens. Some room renters will want to bring furniture but I found them to be less common than those with very little or no furniture. Keep in mind, if tenants are moving their furniture into and out of your home, they may create more wear and tear as they bang walls and door jams moving their furniture in and out and arranging it in the room.

The room I rent now is fully furnished with a quality queen-sized bed with linens, comforter and pillows; a very nice desk with hutch and chair; night stand with lamp and clock; side table; art on the walls; ceiling fan; blinds and curtains. There's no dresser but the medium-size walk-in closet has plenty of shelving to offset the lack of a dresser.

I added to the room while looking at it through the eyes of a tenant. I found that the room became homier and more attractive as I added to it. I actually increased my competitive edge by furnishing and decorating the room.

After observing how tenants used the room, I realized the room needed a small table and chair. Once I added it, I noticed that all the tenants spent a great deal of time at that table. Later I replaced the table with a nice desk, hutch, and a more comfortable chair. As a result, the value of the room grew exponentially to tenants. I strongly recommend including at least a small table and chair or better yet, a desk and chair. It makes the room much more comfortable and functional for the tenant.

If you choose to furnish a bed, make it the best quality you can afford. Most prospective tenants are concerned about the comfort and quality of the bed. A quality bed will make the room more competitive and will attract higher quality tenants.

One note of caution: If you provide a bed, put a quality waterproof mattress cover over the mattress. (Not one of those cheap ones that makes a plastic rustling sound.) The quality covers can be found at mattress stores. The money you invest in a quality cover will be well worth the protection it provides to the mattress. Accidents happen, which can stain mattresses. No one likes to sleep on a stained mattress, and it will be uncovered the first time the tenant washes his sheets.

One tenant spilled a glass of red wine on the bed. The mattress would have had a large, ugly stain that looked like blood if it hadn't been protected by the mattress cover. Of course I subtracted the cost of the ruined mattress cover from his deposit.

When it comes to moving in a tenant's furniture, I learned it was best for my house not to allow it. The few times I did, my doorways and walls got banged up as the tenants moved their furniture in and out and as they used it in their room. I do allow small personal items like an electronic keyboard, TV, stereo and speakers and items of that nature since they won't beat up the room during the moving process or during use.

From another perspective, my mentor friend rents one room furnished and another unfurnished. She doesn't mind the tenants banging up things as they move their furniture in and out of her house. It's a matter of personal preference. Just be aware that a tenant's personal furniture can potentially increase wear and tear on your home.

If you're going to furnish the room, what will you include? How much effort do you want to invest? How much is fiscally feasible? To attract more and higher quality prospects and improve the selection pool, make the room as homey and comfortable as you can afford.

Look at the room as if you're going to rent it. What would you like the room to be like? Consider what a hotel room offers (without the maid service) to make its customers comfortable. Over time you'll find ways to improve the room by talking with prospects, researching the competition and developing experience with tenants.

Most room renters will personalize the room very little. Since the population I've rented to has been overwhelmingly male, tenants have usually brought in a bigger TV than I offered. Few put small personal items on a table. Fewer put small pictures on the wall.

This aspect of renting a room is something that develops over time through a combination of research, budget, available furniture and personal taste.

If you'd like to furnish the room more than you can currently afford, consider asking friends or relatives if they have furniture they want to get off their hands. Maybe they're buying something new or storing furniture in storage units or garages. You can check out garage and yard sales to find fixtures for the room. I found an excellent matching comforter, sheets, pillows cases, and curtains at a neighbor's yard sale as well as a great lamp for the night stand. Furnishing the room can actually be fun with a little creativity and the right frame of mind.

Room Characteristics

What type of closet does the room have, and how much space does it offer a tenant? Closets with adequate space are important to tenants. It is also important that a tenant has the entire closet and doesn't have to share it. It's best to move your personal items out so they are not taking up space in the room the tenant is paying for.

Consider the location of the room within your house. Is the room upstairs or downstairs? Does the room's location provide peace and quiet or is it noisy? Are the windows large or small? Is the room light or dark? Is there a view? How large (or small) is the bedroom? Will it be comfortable for the tenant to spend most of his time in that room? Is there a separate entrance? How much privacy does the room offer? The more privacy you can offer, the more attractive the room will be.

The room I rent is on the far end of the house, opposite from my bedroom and the kitchen. The tenant is the only resident using the bathroom at that end of the house, although occasionally my personal guests may use it. It's also directly next to the bedroom, so the tenant only walks two steps from his room to the bathroom. Tenants love the privacy. Prospects love the idea of the privacy.

The All-Important Bathroom

Bathrooms are important to tenants. Does the room have an attached bathroom, or is it close to a bathroom? Is the bathroom in good or poor condition? Does it have a bath tub or a walk-in shower? Is the toilet old, corroded and/or stained? (You'd be surprised at how important that can be to prospective tenants.) Does it have adequate counter and cupboard space? Is there adequate space for a renter's personal items? Will you provide towels? (Most tenants have their own.) Is it decorated or plain? Is it tiny or roomy? The larger the bathroom, the more attractive it will be to the tenant.

Having a bathroom to themselves is also extremely important to tenants. It can be a deal breaker for some if the bathroom is shared with other household members. The bathroom being in close proximity to the bedroom is another plus. Having to walk through the house to get to the bathroom will be a negative for a prospective tenant. Wouldn't it be to you?

Let's Talk Kitchen

For some, the kitchen will be important. For some, it will be meaningless. Is the kitchen fully equipped with pots/pans, plates, bowls, cutlery, knives, cutting boards, cooking implements, spices, and other common equipment? Does it have a water filter, dishwasher, microwave, or a breakfast nook? Is it small, large, updated or outdated? What is the condition of the refrigerator? How much space will the tenant have in the refrigerator and pantry?

Do you like a neat, orderly kitchen? Are you comfortable with dirty dishes left in the sink or on the counter? My mentor friend doesn't mind tenants waiting a day or two to get to their dishes. I require dishes to be cleaned up within a short period of time. Set up these expectations in advance.

What are the kitchen's features? Even though they are likely to be lightly used if at all, having kitchen privileges without having to contribute to the kitchen is an important attractor factor. Tenants are always relieved to know they can use a fully equipped kitchen and don't need to have kitchen items themselves.

On the other hand, will you want to restrict use of certain items like special dish sets or expensive pots and pans? Will you want the tenant to guarantee that he will be responsible for damages? One thing I make clear in my Agreements Addendum is that if the tenant ruins something he uses, he is expected to replace it immediately. With privileges come responsibilities.

One of my tenants was learning how to cook while living in my house. Early in his cooking adventures he got distracted and badly burnt one of my high quality pans. He was very conciliatory about its destruction. He was surprised when I didn't get upset and equally surprised when I expected him to replace it immediately. When he had to shell out the dough for the pricey pan, he was especially careful of *all* my kitchen items and equipment thereafter. Take heed of the moral of this story. Set expectations in the beginning and follow through when necessary.

Other Privileges
Will you allow dining room privileges? It increases the perceived value of your offering, and most tenants will rarely use the dining room. My tenants usually eat in the privacy of their rooms, perhaps because I expect them to clean up after themselves right away.

Prospective tenants highly value laundry privileges. In fact, the lack of laundry privileges will be a deal killer for many prospects. If you have a washer and dryer, plan to make it available to the tenant.

Don't worry about them getting over used. Most tenants will not use the washer and dryer very much, despite the laundry privileges being such a high value feature. Regardless of this fact, protect your appliances. In the Agreements Addendum, outline the allowable frequency of use and expected care of the facilities (like cleaning out the lint trap and not overloading the machines). Then reinforce it.

Are there other areas of your home that you'll allow a tenant to use on a limited basis? How limited? You define it. Do you have a yard with nice landscaping that the tenant might like to relax in? What about a patio, library, study, bonus room, or a TV room? I allow tenants to use a study/library, covered patio and back yard. I also expect them to take all personal items with them when they leave those areas.

You can decide if these features of your home are available to a tenant per a prearranged basis set forth in the Agreements Addendum. It all depends where you fall on the spectrum between need for privacy and social interaction. The more privileges you allow, the more you will increase the perceived value of your offering.

See the "Preparing for a Renter" section in Chapter 3 for specific aspects that will increase and decrease the value of your room rental.

How Much Do You Want to Share?

How much are you willing or able to share your living space? What do you want to keep to yourself? Will you allow the tenant to be in other parts of the house when you're not around? It is important that you consider your answers. Go back to your needs list. Look at your offering through the eyes of a prospective tenant. The beauty of renting a room over having a roommate is you get to design the living arrangement to suit you. This will change from time to time, and it will evolve over time as you gain experience.

CHAPTER 3

SECRETS TO ATTRACTING
HIGH QUALITY RENTERS

At first, I was only interested in filling the room and collecting the money. As a variety of tenants passed through my home, it became obvious some were easier to live with than others. Some were higher functioning, more considerate, and more compliant than others. Some I liked having around; some I didn't.

As I communicated with a large number of prospective tenants via email, phone and face-to-face interviews, it became apparent there was a huge range of communication and life skills among them. Some people are prone to drama and ongoing problems. Others find it difficult to make rent or will have less-than-desirable guests around, while others can be downright strange. To create a comfortable and profitable experience renting a room, it's important to steer away from these types and attract the more stable, higher functioning people with good relationship, communication and life skills. The lessons from this book will ensure you do.

Just as there are a wide range of prospective tenants looking for a room rental arrangement, there are a wide range of people renting rooms in their homes. Spend some time researching Craigslist. You will find that you have lots of competition out there. This business arrangement is affected by supply and demand, just like any other business. There are plenty of rooms for rent and a limited supply of *quality* tenants. Fortunately, most of the competition doesn't know how to distinguish between the different types of prospects.

If you read the ads on Craigslist, you will see that there is a wide range of professionalism and savvy, or lack of it, in the room renting market. Tenants and prospective tenants tell stories about the range of landlords and prospective landlords. Many landlords have no clue how to rent out a room or how to treat their tenants.

To make renting a room in your house a positive experience for both parties, it is important to attract the right tenants for *you*. If you rent to the right tenants, the experience will be more comfortable and profitable, but finding the right tenant requires a competitive edge. You can create that edge by learning about the process of renting a room and by presenting your home, yourself and your rental arrangement with confidence and professionalism.

Another component of increasing your competitive edge and attracting higher quality tenants is that you have to provide an appealing room. The more you add and the nicer you make the room, the more people are going to be interested in it, which means a larger pool of prospects to choose from. If you present a shabby or too sparse room, you may end up with fewer prospects and accepting less than desirable renters. The key here is YOU choose.

Price is another important factor in attracting quality renters. If you charge too little rent, you will attract financially troubled people or cheapskates. If you charge too much, you can price yourself out of the market. Pricing the room appropriately will take research and a bit of trial and error, but it is an important factor in getting the right people.

Don't be afraid to set expectations for the tenants' behavior and how they treat your home. If you set no or low expectations, the tenants will live down to meet them. By setting higher expectations (and reinforcing them) you will improve the type of tenants who are willing to consider your rental arrangement. You want tenants who are *capable* of living up to your expectations.

Conducting the tenant search and interview and presenting yourself, your home and your room rental arrangement with professionalism will attract the higher quality tenant and discourage the lower functioning ones. If a prospect is bothered by your professional approach, you have screened him out because he has revealed he wants to be the one in charge.

Preparing for a Renter

Making Room
The first thing you need to do is make room for the renter. Clean out the bedroom and the tenant's bathroom. Remove your personal effects and find other places for them. For most people, this means rearranging parts of the rest of your house to accommodate the belongings that were in the bedroom and bathroom you will be renting. Sometimes you may have to consolidate and

let go of "stuff" you don't really need and don't have room for anymore.

Next, you need to make room in the refrigerator and pantry for the tenant. For many tenants, having adequate space in the refrigerator and pantry are important, even if most won't cook much. In the refrigerator, you should give the tenant a shelf or two, a rack or two in the door and maybe a drawer. Clear out adequate space in the pantry to store cereal boxes and miscellaneous food items (maybe two-and-a-half to three feet of shelf space on two to three shelves). What you offer depends on your pantry size, cupboard space and refrigerator and is always negotiated with the tenant.

You will probably have to rearrange your use of the refrigerator and pantry. You may need to store less food to accommodate space for the tenant. At first I thought this was an unpleasant inconvenience, but it forced me to be more efficient with my food purchases and storage. However, most of my tenants have used less space than I allotted. A few used no room at all in the refrigerator and pantry.

If you allow dining room, laundry or other privileges, you may need to clean up clutter in these areas to make room for the tenant's use. Again, this will entail finding other places for or consolidating belongings that will get in the way of the tenant using the privileged areas.

Don't over think making room, just do it. If this type of activity is painful for you, find someone to help with it. Remember, you're not made of china. You'll get used to the new arrangement.

What Exactly Will You Offer and Allow?

How much of your home do you want to share and under what circumstances? What type of privileges are you going to allow?

What's the shortest rental term you will allow? There will be prospects that want to rent the room for a few weeks or a month. They're looking for a hotel situation in your home. I require a minimum of three months to make it worth my while to go through the time and trouble of searching for a renter. What is the shortest length of time that will make it worth your while? As you gain experience, your thoughts on this may evolve.

Parking

All tenants are concerned about where they will park their cars. They will be concerned about safety and convenience. You may have to do some rearranging so the tenant can park in a safe, convenient place.

Some tenants will expect to park in the garage. This is not a reasonable expectation, though some landlords will allow it. Most apartments charge an extra fee for a garage. When tenants pay the full expense of renting an entire house, a garage is part of the expense and added responsibilities of a house.

At one time one of my tenants had a Jaguar. He knew he would only be renting for three or four months. Since he knew the situation was temporary, he didn't mind parking on the street in front of my home for that short time period. The short-term tenants know their situation is temporary, and they will tend not to view parking as a high priority.

If there is room in the garage for a tenant's car, do you want to charge an extra fee for the convenience? Consider how much it would be worth to you to accommodate another car in the garage? Is it worth another source of revenue?

All of this is assuming you live in an area where parking is a given. In some metropolitan areas, parking is a premium or a luxury. If this is true for you, convenient and/or free parking may not be something a tenant can reasonably expect. Charging garage rent for non-tenants could be an additional source of income.

Garage Use

Some tenants will want to store belongings in the garage. This is an area of personal preference. Do you need to rearrange things in your garage to accommodate space for a tenant? Do you want to charge extra for storage? Will you allow the tenant to store a small amount of personal items?

My mentor friend allows tenants to store items free of charge in her garage. I do not, except for a bike or a small item or two. Garage use will come up with tenants, so this is an area that requires consideration.

Will You Allow the Tenant to Eat in His Room?

While doing my research, I read many competing landlords' ads in which the landlords forbade tenants to eat in their rooms.

I have always allowed tenants to eat in the rented room. Room renters tend to be private people who like the privacy and convenience of eating in their rooms. Many prospective tenants would consider it a drawback if they were restricted to only eating in the kitchen or dining room.

I have not had any problems with stale food drawing rodents or creating odors in the rented room, because I set clear boundaries upfront about not leaving food in the bedroom. I also include a few sentences about it in my Agreements Addendum.

Some people have voiced concerns about tenants leaving food or beverage stains in the rented bedroom. By requiring a deposit and enforcing the move out procedures (both discussed in "Managing the Relationship with the Tenant" and "Nuts and Bolts"), you will indirectly persuade tenants to take care of the spaces they are renting.

Pricing the Room

As in any business, correctly pricing your commodity is crucial. Also as in any business, you need to research the competition, analyze what the market will bear and learn from some trial and error to get the price right. What the housing market will bear in different cities will vary widely. Renting a room in San Jose will fetch a higher amount than in San Antonio.

The best and easiest way to get an idea of what you should charge is to get on Craigslist. Research what the competition is charging. There are hundreds of ads with a wide variety of offerings and prices.

Once you research competitors' ads, you will better understand the room renter market in your area. Most ads lack sophistication and professionalism. It will be obvious that most of the competition doesn't know what they're doing. Following the advice in this manual will set you way ahead of your competition.

Go to www.craigslist.com. Choose your city (or the city closest to you). Find the "Housing" heading and then "Rooms/Share." This is your competition. These are the people vying for the same tenants. Most ads reflect a minimum of effort invested. Some are barely literate. Most are poorly written.

You will notice that some features increase the value of a room rental offering and some decrease it. For starters, here's a list of aspects that will increase the value of an offering:

- Private entrance or an entrance that reduces the tenant's interaction with the landlord/family
- Easy access to major roads, highways or thoroughfares
- Near major places like large employers, universities, medical centers
- Close to stores, shops, gyms, restaurants, etc.
- Amenities like cable TV and internet
- Neat, clean house and/or yard
- Safe and/or quiet neighborhoods
- Room fan (in warm climates)
- Good-size to large bedroom
- Good-size to large closet
- Plenty of privacy
- Private bathroom
- Very few people in the house
- Furnished, either partially or fully
- TV (though tenants will likely bring in a large one of their own)
- Privileges (like kitchen, laundry, dining)

- Access to other parts of the house that are unused or seldom used

If you offer some of these features, you will be able to charge a higher rent. Some features will increase your "curb appeal," which will in turn increase confidence in what you are offering; as a result, you will attract higher quality renters.

Here are some aspects that will decrease the value to a potential tenant. If your offering contains some of these items, don't worry; it won't kill your ability to rent the room. You may have to price the room a little lower or add amenities to compensate for these negative aspects:

- No cable or internet (most renters require at least internet)
- Shared bathroom
- Poorly maintained bathroom
- Dirty or messy house
- House and/or yard in poor condition
- More than two other people in the house
- Other room renters
- Children and/or pets (for some)
- Located on a busy street
- Small bedroom
- Small closet
- Less privacy (other resident bedrooms are close to the renter's room)
- Lack of, or restricted privileges (no laundry or very restrictive kitchen privileges)
- Inconvenient location
- Far from stores, shops, restaurants, gyms, etc.

It will take you a little time to get the price just right. If you price it too low, you will attract more responses, but you will attract many low quality renters. One problem with too many responses from lower quality renters is the amount of time you will spend responding to emails, talking on the phone and meeting face-to-face with potential tenants.

You can waste a lot of time and energy wading through a list of people with minimal life and communication skills as well as challenge your patience and nerves. Remember, people with lower life and communication skills are going to use those lackluster skills in their living environments.

If you price your offering too high, you will restrict the amount of responses. When people do come for the face-to-face interview and see the offering, they will lose interest, which also wastes your time.

If time is on your side and you don't urgently need the additional income, you can take the time to hold to your price and wait until the right person comes along. If time is of the essence and you urgently need additional income, you may need to lower the price to increase responses and speed up the process of filling the vacancy.

If you have the luxury of time, you can experiment with different price ranges. One week you can place the ad for one price, and then the next week advertise another price. The week after that, you can try a third price. The challenge is keeping straight the price you offered as you talk or visit with prospective tenants. When I did this, I asked the respondents what price was listed in the ad they were responding to. If they didn't remember, I quoted them the higher price.

Experiment with price and what you offer over time. Add or remove amenities. Reduce or increase privileges. Fix problem areas. Adjust this or that as you gain experience over time. The adjustments may alter what you can charge or they may make the price more attractive. In the end, research, combined with trial and error, will get the pricing just right.

CHAPTER 4

FINDING RENTERS

Sources for Finding Renters

There are a variety of sources for finding renters. You need to generate a sufficient volume of responses to find the right person. You will have to wade through many calls and emails and a fair amount of face-to-face interviews before you can find the right fit. The more responses you receive, the more options you have, and the more likely that you will find the right fit.

Time is a very important factor to consider when advertising for a tenant. Advertising sources need to be cost effective in the time it takes to create them. Finding a tenant can be time consuming, and the time invested needs to be effective.

It will take you time to create advertising whether it's online, for the newspaper, a flyer, an email or conversations with your circle of friends. It will take you time to field the responses. You have to read and respond to emails. You have to field phone calls. You will have to talk to a wide variety of people on the phone and face-to-face. If your advertising generates responses from undesirable types of people, you waste valuable time. If your advertising isn't generating sufficient responses, you waste the time invested in creating and maintaining the ad.

Here is a thorough list of places you might consider advertising. You may come up with some others as well.

Craigslist – www.craigslist.com
Craigslist is free. It's easy to post an ad. It's heavily used by prospective tenants. If you write the ad properly, it will generate a generous volume of responses. On Craigslist, you can make the ad as thorough as necessary, which will filter out inappropriate tenants and attract the desirable ones.

The best advertising makes the most effective use of time by attracting the right kind of prospects (and enough of them) for the least amount of money. In my experience, Craigslist has been by far the most effective means for finding tenants.

By following the instructions in "The Ins and Outs of Craigslist" below, you will set yourself apart from the competition and attract a sufficient volume of *appropriate* prospects from which to choose a tenant.

Word of Mouth
This is not terribly effective, but it could be an option. Timing is everything. Perhaps someone you know knows someone

who's looking right at the time you have a vacancy. If the living situation gets rough or doesn't work out, you may experience potential awkwardness in your circle of acquaintances/family/ friends.

Flyers at Colleges, Stores and Other Locations

Another not terribly effective source, but it could be an option. Of all the flyers I put up at colleges and stores, I received few calls. This might be a supplement.

Want Ads in the Newspaper

These are very pricey and don't provide enough bang for the buck. You are limited to only a few lines in a newspaper ad. It's not possible to effectively screen for the desired type of person because of the limited amount of ad space. You will need to run the ad continually to obtain a sufficient amount of calls. This is an expensive way to attract a lot of inappropriate prospects, which wastes time and wears you out.

There are also those penny-saver publications. Keep in mind, their target market is people who are *penny-saver* oriented. They are for folks who don't want to pay much for anything. Do you really want cheap skates or the financially strapped responding to your ad or renting your room?

Roomster.Com and Other For-Fee Tenant-Finding Websites

These websites might be effective in a town where they are actually used. I've tried them, and they generated few responses in my town, San Antonio, the seventh largest city in the country. Even if these sites had been free, I wasted the time I spent getting signed up because of the limited responses. Perhaps you might have better luck than I did.

College Websites

Some colleges have electronic boards for students looking for a roommate or room rental. If you live near a college or university, check their website to see if they have such an electronic board and if they allow non-students to use it. When I used the electronic board for the college near me, I received very few responses.

Ins and Outs of Craigslist

There is an art and science to using Craigslist effectively for renting a room. If you learn the techniques for successfully navigating Craigslist, you will be able to hit the ground running for finding the right tenants.

Consistently Post Ads

I learned from prospective tenants' feedback that they only look back two to three days in the ads. With so many people posting ads on Craigslist every day, yours will quickly get lost among the dozens, if not hundreds. Therefore, you need to refresh the ad every two to three days. If you let the intervals go longer, the responses will dry up.

Some days you will receive only one or two responses. Some days you will get five or six, while some days you will only hear from scammers. If you are diligent in refreshing the ad, you will overcome the unpredictable nature of ad responses. If you are lack luster about changing up the ad, you will create an uneven flow of responses.

The Ebb and Flow
The stream of responses has a cyclic nature. It will ebb and flow with certain times of the month and year. If you understand this ebb and flow, you can prevent getting discouraged, maintain your patience, and develop a better sense of timing.

Middle of the Month
The largest volume of responses comes at this time. Most people have living arrangements that require vacating by end of the month; many prospective renters are busy looking during this time for an end-of-the month change. Room renters are not always well-organized folks and last minute can tend to rule.

End of the Month
Many people looking at this time are under pressure because they haven't yet found a place to live. They are likely the disorganized ones who haven't been looking diligently (if at all) until the last minute. They will want to move quickly and don't really care much about where they live.

First of the Month
Many searchers will have found places by end of the month. You will experience a slowdown in responses after the first

of the month. The renters that are looking at this time are likely more organized and are generally *not* in a hurry. These people will tend to be real shoppers because they have more time, and they will scrutinize every aspect of a prospective landlord's offering.

Holidays and Winter Months

Inclement weather and the distractions of holiday seasons tend to discourage moving during this time of year. However, that doesn't mean that no one moves. You will still have some people looking, but you will experience a smaller volume of responses than you would usually receive in the summer.

There is an exception. If you live in a college town, there will be some activity during the winter break when students attempt to move before the next semester or quarter begins. You may want to keep track of the semester/quarter break periods for the college(s) in your town.

Late Spring through End of Summer

This tends to be the busiest time for relocations. You will notice a strong flurry of activity a few weeks to a month before the fall semester or quarter begins for college.

When I first started renting a room, I found information about seasonal changes helpful. At one point I was getting worried about the low volume of responses at the beginning of the month. I discussed it with my mentor friend, and she advised me to hold on, because once the month wore on, more responses would roll in. Over time I started to see the pattern described above unfold.

One Caveat

In locations where it is generally mild in the winter and hot as hell in the summer, the ebb and flow is likely to be reversed. It can tend to be busier in the winter and slower in the summer.

Weekends, Week Days and Evenings

You will probably notice a much higher volume of email and phone responses on the weekend. Many prospective renters will want to see the place and meet you face-to-face during the weekends. Mondays and Tuesdays tend to be the slowest time for responses. Many prospects are researching housing after work, so they will send a majority of emails in the evenings. Stay on top of emails during the weekend and evening or first thing in the morning.

Posting Ads on Craigslist

Technology changes and improves continually. Instructions I wrote for posting ads on Craigslist were outdated within a few months of writing them. Due to the fast moving nature of the internet, for the most current instructions on posting ads to Craigslist, go to their FAQ section. The instructions are clear and easy to follow.

To create a steady stream of responses, you need to post regular fresh ads every two to three days. Dozens of landlords are posting ads every day, and your ad will be buried within a few days. By posting a new ad, it will go to the top of the list.

Fresh ads will get more viewings, but if you don't have time to post a new ad, at least take time to re-post your current ad.

Changing the ad and its title and making them look a little different will attract prospects that may have passed up the ad on a previous occasion. Prospects have told me many times that they responded to my ad because they kept seeing it in various forms.

Over time I wrote up to 20 ads with different titles, and I varied them enough so that they might attract a prospect that passed it up on a previous day. As time goes on and you adjust your offering, you'll also adjust the ads to reflect the changes.

Start out with five to ten ads. Write a basic ad and then vary it in format or wording. (I'll show you how.) Create one document with all the ads and their subject lines. Above each ad type in *red italics* the date the ad is run. Keep track of when you ran the ad so you know when you can run it again. It also helps to track the success rate of each ad.

It's important to invest some time and energy in creating the ads. Essentially, you need to write ad copy to attract prospects. You have to write good ads and keep them rolling if you want to attract quality tenants.

Scams

In every business enterprise there are going to be scams and would-be scammers. It's no different for renting a room in your home. By becoming familiar with the modus operandi, you will know not to take them seriously, you won't waste time engaging with them, and most importantly, you won't fall prey to them.

The scams usually come from emails with the purpose of deceiving the reader into cashing a bogus cashier's check and wiring the scammer money. The emails contain typical telltale signs. The signs that are specific to renting a room ads are thoroughly discussed in Appendix A. Craigslist's website also has an analysis of general scams under "Avoid Scams and Fraud." Take time to review these sections. It's critical that you are educated about them before they start bombarding you. It's important to be ready for them.

Creating Ads That Attract Quality Renters

To follow the discussion below, go to www.craigslist.com. Choose your city or the city closest to you. Find the "Housing" heading and then "Rooms/Share," then chose "Post."

Process Basics

When creating a post for a room rental (the ad), the post requires a Title. You want to write a title that will catch the prospect's eye. Next you need to enter your Description. Simply cut and paste the current ad from your list of pre-written ads. By labeling each ad with dates as described above, you can simply and quickly know which one is next.

After you have entered your Description, you have the option to enter your Street, Nearest Cross Street, City and State. All of these are optional. Never give the street number. You don't want any weirdoes showing up at your door or casing the joint because you published the specific address. The more information you provide, the more details the prospective tenant has about the home's location. It's not necessary to include street name and cross streets in the Location section of the title or in the actual description.

Construction Basics

It only takes 15 minutes of reading competitors' ads to realize you will set yourself apart if you

- use correct spelling and grammar,
- are succinct and clear,
- are interesting and fun.

I am constantly amazed at how badly written many of the ads are. If you know that your writing skills are challenged, enlist the aid of a friend or trade services with someone who can edit or clean up the ad copy. Make every possible effort to post literate ad copy.

Example Ad

I have included an example of one of my ads below. In Appendix B there are ten other examples. Feel free to plagiarize the ads.

Title: $500 Furnished Room Plus Lots of Extras

$500 Fully Furnished Room in a Cozy, Homey House.
It includes -

- Nice, light, good size room with walk-in closet with lots of shelving
- The room is on the opposite side of the house from my bedroom so it's like you have one side of the house to yourself
- High quality queen-size bed with bedding (you just need your own pillows)

- Large desk with large hutch, chair, table, TV, bedside table, ceiling fan and other useful miscellaneous items (see pictures)
- Large bathroom all to yourself. It has ample drawer/cupboard space, towels, tub/shower and is located just off the bedroom so there's lots of privacy
- All utilities, cable and wireless internet included ($200 equivalent)
- Most housekeeping and all yard work are included
- Privileges for: kitchen (fully equipped with everything you need – except your food), dining room and laundry (I provide the detergents, etc.)
- Shared access to screened-in porch, which looks out into a wooded area and library/study room for hanging out

Best Suited for Temporary Resident of Three to Six Months Duration.

The house is:

- A nice one-story, 1900-square-foot home in XXXXXX subdivision off (major cross roads) down from the Wash Tub and Post Office on (major street near my home).
- In a safe, secluded, quiet, friendly, heavily-treed neighborhood
- One block from a lovely green belt
- Close to lots of parks, hiking, walking as well as stores/shops and restaurants
- A few blocks from a bus stop, with lots of other bus stops in the neighborhood
- Near the Medical Center area, UTSA and USAA; Easy, 5-7 minute access to (major cross roads), yet neighborhood is nice and secluded

Also, living in my home are 2 mellow cats and a small dog (walked two times a day) – all are indoor/outdoor and well behaved, so a renter without pets is a must. No worries, there's no odor and no pet hair because there is a pet door to the outside and no kitty litter indoors. Plus, I keep the house vacuumed and dusted.

I'm looking for one person who is

- Quiet
- Drug and smoke free
- Easy on the drinking and partying

I am:

- Quiet and responsible
- Fitness and outdoor –oriented
- Single, business woman

Requirements to move in:

- 1st month's rent - $500 (or prorated amount if moving in after the 1st)
- Deposit - $200
- Month to month rental agreement – signed

Please respond to XXXXXXX@XXXX.com. I will reply with an invitation to my Photo album. If you like what you see we can talk.

Writing the Ads
Refer to Appendix B for a template to help customize your own ads.

Describe what is included in the room rental:

- Describe the bedroom and possibly its location within the home
- Describe bedroom furnishings
- Describe the bathroom (always important to renters)
- Shared rooms or areas of your home
- Identify privileges (like kitchen, laundry room, dining room)
- Clarify if bills are included (which ones and how much they're worth)
- Other amenities

If it's important to have a long-term or short-term renter, mention it.

Describe the strengths of your home and the surrounding area:

- One- or two-story and square footage of home
- List major cross roads (optional if you want to list subdivision)
- Features of the neighborhood (safe, secluded, near stores, parks)
- List nearby points of interest (university, hospital, major employers, theme parks, downtown)
- List access to major roads or highways
- Accessibility to public transit, which is important to some renters
- Other aspects that make it attractive

Briefly describe the type of person you are looking for:

- Partier/No partying
- Social/Quiet

- Pets okay/No pets
- Smoking okay/No smoking
- One person, couple, kids okay
- Other aspects

Briefly tell about yourself:

- Single or married couple
- Working person or retired
- Male or female
- A few other brief aspects

Tell about pets or children in the home:

- Children – tell their ages and gender
- Children – tell a little about them: well behaved, respectful of renter's privacy, busy with after school activities, gone every other weekend, etc.
- Pets – quantity and types of animals
- Pets – reassure prospects they are well behaved and the house is kept free of hair and odor (always a concern for renters)

Conclude by telling them about:

- The photo album
- Type of agreement
- Cost of moving in
- Your email address

Pictures Are Essential

Through your research you will notice that many ads on Craigslist don't contain pictures. It takes time and effort to take, upload and post pictures. Most of the competitors aren't going to invest the time. The few ads that do contain pictures frequently don't show well.

Shopping for a room rental is a task that engages only one of the five senses: the visual sense. It's a lopsided task that doesn't fully engage the senses and can be a drudge for many shoppers. By including pictures, you add depth and breadth to the visual process and makes your ad more appealing. Think of it like a dating website. The more and better pictures you provide, the more you improve your chances of finding the right person.

Since pictures can show poorly on Craigslist, and it can take a lot of time to post as many as you need to, the best way to create a visual depiction of your offering is to create a web album.

Create a Web Album

Once you have cleaned up, organized and furnished the room, take pictures of the entire offering, upload them to a computer and create a free, secure online photo album. You will share this album via email with prospective tenants so they can view it before a phone conversation and face-to-face interview.

By looking through your pictures, prospects will be able to get a good visual idea of what you are offering and if it meets their needs. It's an excellent screening tool. Prospects will decide if they want to pursue their interest in the room or move on to a competing room.

You need to put enough time and energy into your pictures so you create a thorough exhibit of your offering. If you create a photo album that shows the offering well, you will engage and entice more prospective tenants to follow up for at least a phone conversation, if not a face-to-face interview. People tend to be very visual; seeing what they may be getting themselves into is important to most prospective tenants.

Take pictures of different angles of the room, the closet, the bathroom, the kitchen, dining room, laundry facilities (if you choose to allow privileges), front of the house, the back yard, the entrance hall or private entrance, and any other parts of the house they'll have access to. Create a thorough visual. Show off all the aspects of your home that you are sharing.

It may seem like common sense (or maybe not), but tidy up before taking the pictures. Pictures of a messy house will show the house badly and will contradict the reason you have pictures.

Do not scrimp on time or energy for this project. It's too important to do in half measures. Bear in mind, this only has to be done once, and then you can freshen up the album from time to time when you make changes to the room or house.

Some landlords will include pictures in their Craigslist ads. Pictures can show poorly on Craigslist. It's a slow process to upload pictures and you need to repost the ad every two or three days. Uploading pictures every time will be time-prohibitive. Pictures in a web album always look far superior to the ones in the Craigslist ads. In addition, the web album is quick and easy to forward to a prospect.

If prospects find your listing interesting enough, they will send an email. At that time prospects will request to view the photo album mentioned in the ad, or you can volunteer to send it. You will send an invitation to view the album, and prospects will contact you again if they like what they see.

To get some ideas of how to show the room in pictorial format, and mostly what not to do, research ads on Craigslist to see what the competition has done. I have generated consistent, excellent results with my web albums. Whenever prospects viewed them, they invariably pursued the next level of contact.

Most landlords (the competition) are not going to put much, if any, effort into the photos of their offerings. Remember, this is a business proposition with others competing for the same renters. Creating a photo album that attractively depicts your offering is one of the key components to setting yourself apart.

One additional perk to having a web album of the offering is you will have pictorial evidence of everything that was in the room and home before a tenant moved in. This came in handy when one of my tenants moved out and took an item from the room that he genuinely believed he had brought with him. By showing him the photo album, he realized the item was indeed mine and returned it promptly. The web album will create the same protection for you as well.

Not technically savvy? Don't know how to take digital pictures or upload them to a computer? Haven't ever created a web album? Well, now's the time to stretch, grow and learn some new skills. Borrow a camera. Learn how to use the camera on your phone. Trade dinner or trade one of your skills with a friend or acquaintance who possesses the required skills. Do what it takes to make this part of the process work. It is essential to being competitive.

Web Album Options

There are a variety of free web album options on the internet. Since I use Gmail for my tenant search, I use its free web album option. You can find similar free web albums for Yahoo, Hotmail and possibly the email service you use.

I find Gmail's web album option very easy and quick to use (and the receiver doesn't need to have a Gmail account). Create a free Gmail account. Log into it. Click the "More" tab at the top, then choose "Photos." Follow the directions for creating an album and uploading photos. Remember, you only have to do this once, and then you can freshen up the album from time to time when you make changes to the room or house.

When I want to email the album to a prospect, I click on the album, choose "Share" and cut and paste the prospect's email address into the "To" box. I write a note in the "Message" box. Hit "Share Via Email" and off it goes.

There are plenty of free web album websites that require users to have accounts. If the prospect doesn't have an account, it may be too much trouble to set one up just to view the album. The key is "easy." It's easy to scroll through the pictures in an emailed web album. Make it easy for the prospects or they will move on to the competition.

Separate Dedicated Email Address

Create a separate dedicated email address for this process. Think of it as your business email for renting a room. With the volume of wanted and unwanted email we all receive, it's easy to lose track of important emails, like prospective renter responses.

A separate, dedicated email makes it easier and simpler to manage the inevitable back and forth email communication efficiently. It will contain all of the room rental email traffic to one place and reduce the opportunities to lose or miss a prospective renter's email.

Unfortunately, another slew of emails come with running an ad for renting a room. There are scam, solicitation and a variety of spam emails. These will be contained to the room-renting-email and will not be added to the volume you probably already receive in your personal email.

The unwanted emails will come while the email is dormant until you use it again for the next round of ads and tenant hunting. Better to contain those unwanted emails in the dedicated email instead of being bombarded in your usual personal email.

Creating a separate dedicated email is quick, easy and free. What's better than that? You can create multiple email addresses on many different sites: Gmail, Hotmail, and Yahoo to name a few. Choose a simple email address that doesn't have any racy or discriminatory connotations.

Using Craigslist's Email Versus Your Own

Craigslist encourages communication through their system and discourages using your own email address. They contend that you may attract scammers and other unsolicited emails if you post your own email address.

When I use my own email address, I do get more scammers and unsolicited emails. On the other hand, when I respond to a prospect that used Craigslist's communication system, my email consistently does not get through to the prospect. Despite the annoyance of scammer or unsolicited email, use your own room-renter designated email address.

CHAPTER 5

TENANT SELECTION AND SCREENING PROCESS

The previous section was about bringing in the fish. This section is about cleaning them.

Selection Process

It isn't difficult to find a tenant. There are lots of people looking for rooms and lots of people offering to rent rooms. You need some finesse in the selection and screening process to find a *quality* tenant compatible with your preferences.

You have two objectives in the selection and screening process. The first is to find a quality renter who will co-create a good experience for you. The second is to make you stand out among the others offering rooms for rent, often for less money. To accomplish these objectives there is a process with specific steps.

Step 1- Emails

First, the prospect will send an email of interest about the ad. It's important to respond within 24 hours or less to all serious emails.

If you wait a few days to respond, you will lose excellent prospects. These are leads. You must pounce on them quickly while they're still hot. Prospective renters' interest will cool quickly, because other ads, other prospective landlords and other prospective homes will entice them. Many prospective renters will make decisions quickly.

A range of emails from scams to spam to possible to impossible prospects will flow into and sometimes flood your email. To keep up and stay organized, create a folder in your In Box specifically for prospects. When you receive responses from good prospects, move their emails to that special folder. If you ensure that those emails are easily accessible, it will be simpler to follow up with prospects.

The first time you respond to an inquiry, send the prospect a link to the photo album so he can see the offering, or ask him if he would like to see the photo album. In the first-response emails, you need to sell the offering; you cannot just send bland, careless responses. This is a sales process; you are selling prospects on *engaging in enough contact* to decide if they merit inviting for a visit and interview. Moving *quality* prospects to this step is crucial.

You need to craft short responses to engage attention. Most prospects are emailing multiple potential landlords. There is an abundance of competition for prospective tenants' attention. You need to grab it.

Since home hunters are sending numerous emails, it's common for them to lose track of which ad they may be talking about with you. When responding, add a little information about the place to remind them, essentially selling it. You can include a link to the ad at the bottom of your email. Be friendly and courteous.

Here are a few of my responses to initial inquiries from prospective renters.

The room is still available. I live in the XXXXXXXX subdivision near XXXXX and XXXX. It's a very central location and the subdivision is nicely secluded amid all the hubbub of the area. Here is a link to the photo album of my home.

http://XXXXXXXXXXXXXXXXXXXXXXXXXXX

If you like what you see, give me a call and we can chat and/or you can come by to look at the place.

———

Yes, the room is still available. Would you like to see a photo album of my home?

If you like what you see then we can talk more. Just keep in mind this is a room rental and not a roommate/house share. The ad spells out that rent includes all bills plus the bedroom and a private bathroom. The rental includes shared access to the study/library and screened-in porch plus there are privileges for the kitchen, laundry and dining room. Some folks get confused and think this is a full house share/roommate situation.

Have a great day.

Through trial and error, you will learn what type of responses result in follow-ups from prospects. Feel free to use my responses above; they are tried and true. Cut and paste the same initial response. During busy times of the month, you will be reading and responding to lots of emails. Cutting and pasting the same initial response creates consistency and reduces the time you have to spend processing through them. Of course, customize the response when a prospect asks a question.

You must craft quality responses to move prospects through the process. There are a limited number of quality prospects. By responding quickly and with ample information, you will engage quality prospects and move them to the next step of the process: the phone call.

Texting

Texting is natural (and seemingly essential) to some, especially people in their teens and twenties and those with children of a "texting age." Anyone with children or who knows people with children, understands the convenience and proliferation of this short hand version of communication. However, for communication about important aspects of life, like screening people who may live in your home, it is not an appropriate means of communication. You can't get a good enough feel for people through texting.

People who text about the ad don't understand certain basic life skills and possess minimal standards of behavior. People that text about something as important as their prospective living arrangements generally don't understand (or value) the many spoken and unspoken social rules of living with others. When "texters" have come to my home, they have not been the quality of renter I'm seeking. I have had a few of these individuals as renters. Their lack of skills and manners can create drama, conflict and plain ole annoyances because they don't understand or value common social rules.

Step 2 - The Phone Conversation

When you have found an interesting person through email, the next step is to chat with him over the phone. If I have enough responses where I can be a bit choosy, I will invite the prospect to call me. I like to see if he has the life skills and motivation to follow up, characteristics of quality renters.

The phone call offers you the opportunity to get a feel for the prospect and vice versa. You can easily spot an inappropriate prospect over the phone. There are little tells: they complain a lot, they display attitudes you're not comfortable with, and they talk too much or barely talk at all. They will reveal their manners and life skills in the conversation. There are a variety of things that you can discern about a person over the phone.

The phone conversation also provides the opportunity to have a candid conversation about expectations on both sides. Reiterate this is a room rental and not a house share. Many renters will be looking for the perks of a house share at the lower price and responsibility level of a room rental. It's frustrating when people take up time coming to your home, only to find they are actually looking for a house share.

The phone conversation is also the time when prospects will ask questions, like do you mind a visiting non-custodial son or daughter, a pet, or a smoker. Get these types of qualifying conversations taken care of on the phone, *before* the inappropriate prospects take up time coming to your home.

Some landlords skip the phone conversation phase by inviting the person to the house through email. What you decide is a matter of preference and trust in humanity (and maybe luck). Occasionally I will skip the phone call if an interesting prospect and I can't get our schedules to mesh for a phone conversation. However, skipping the phone call means skipping an important qualifying part of the process, so you may end up wasting time with unqualified prospects.

Step 3 - The House Tour

When you open the door to the prospective tenant for his initial visit, you are both getting your first impression. Pay attention to your reaction and gut feeling about the person. On the other side, remember, this is the prospect's first impression of you too. Set a professional, yet friendly, tone from the outset.

Since you are competing with other prospective landlords for the quality tenant, show the home at its best. Turn on the lights. Open the blinds. Tidy up the place. Make sure the tenant's private area, like the bedroom and bathroom, is clean and neat.

It can be awkward for both parties when an unfamiliar person comes to your home to inspect it and you. Take charge and break the ice by offering to give the tour immediately. By starting the tour immediately, you loosen up the awkwardness and allow conversation to flow. Walking through the house encourages a more natural atmosphere for both of you to ask questions and get a feel for one another. On the tour, the prospective tenant can quickly see if the home will be suitable for him. If it's not, he can cut the visit short and not waste any more of your time or his.

Showing While an Existing Tenant Is Still in Residence

Don't do it. It's an invasion of the existing tenant's privacy if you are popping in and out of his room with strangers. The bedroom and bathroom will contain the tenant's personal affects and usually the rooms will range from untidy to a disaster area. Prospective renters cannot see beyond the current condition of the room and bathroom and will be turned off. When you show the room and house, it needs to look its best. It will not look its best with the existing tenant still living in it. It's frustrating and a waste of time.

Step 4 - The Interview

As described in the section above, you actually begin the interview during the house tour. After the tour, sit down with the tenant. Be friendly and relaxed but still maintain a professional orientation. Chat. Get to know one another a little. Develop a list of questions you want to know about a prospective tenant. Discuss living habits, likes, and dislikes. Discuss ground rules. I have found that having the Agreements Addendum in hand and using it as a template for the topics I want to cover has worked well. However, at the same time, don't make it seem like an interrogation.

It is your home, so take charge of the discussion. Some tenant prospects will try to take control of the interview. You are the one taking the risk and inviting a stranger into your home. It is your home and your personal property he'll be using, so it's your liability. Stay in charge of the conversation and situation. At the same time, don't dominate it. Find a balance. It will be easier for you to stay in charge during the entire process, including the living situation, if you are in charge from the beginning.

Overtime, you will gain a comfort level and confidence with the interview process. You will develop a style and will identify content that works for you.

Use your intuition or gut during this phase of tenant selection. Listen to the quiet voice. It doesn't shout; that's why it can be easy to ignore. Some people believe intuition is where we connect with Spirit. Some people believe intuition is the subconscious mind trying to communicate the cues and clues it has picked up that the conscious mind has missed. If you don't believe in intuition, listen to your gut instincts and gut reactions. Intuition and your gut will tell you information that later experience will confirm. I guarantee it.

If you reach a comfort level with the prospect, ask what his timeline is and if he is interested in the room. Inform him that you require a completed application for serious consideration. Have one ready with a pen. If the prospect is serious, he will complete the application. If not, he will be on his way. (See "The Paperwork" section in Chapter 6.)

If the prospect expresses interest, inform him that you will halt the search once you receive money for at least the deposit, and that you require a signed month-to-month rental agreement. If you are going to require background or credit checks, now is the time to inform him.

You can extend an invitation to become a tenant at the interview or during a call back afterwards. Don't wait too many days after seeing a prospect to extend the invitation. Other competing landlords are also seeking your prospect's attention.

When to Cut Short the Interview
Occasionally, a prospect will come to the house and be negative. He will criticize you, your home and/or your offering. If you interview enough people, this will happen occasionally. It's highly

inappropriate for a prospect to express negativity or criticism. If this happens, cut the interview short. This person is trying to grab control of the situation and would create a negative experience as a tenant. The selection process takes a lot of time and this type of person is wasting it. Also, it is important that you do not take any of it personally.

You will conduct lots of interviews. This part can take a fair amount of time, especially before you learn to screen out inappropriate candidates. There will be plenty of people who are obviously not right. Sometimes it will be obvious immediately. Sometimes it takes a little time with them. Once it's obvious, cut the interview short.

If you decide to cut an interview short, tell him there are a lot of people coming to see your home and you need to move on to the next upcoming appointment. Tell him you have to be somewhere. Tell him to think it over and get back to you. Tell him whatever feels comfortable. Your time and energy are valuable, and you will tire of spending it on inappropriate tenant prospects.

Eventually, you will refine your radar and you will be able to sense the people who do not match. You'll learn the qualities and characteristics that end up being a good fit and those that are a poor fit. I guarantee some of it will surprise you.

Don't Take Anything Personally
Finding a compatible tenant requires interaction with a wide range of personalities. Don't take any of it personally. No one is thinking enough about anyone else's feelings or reactions to take any part of this process personally. It's a waste of time, energy and imagination.

Working with Out-of-Town Prospects

One type of prospect will be living outside your area planning to relocate. You will communicate with them through email, phone and/or Skype. Sometimes you'll meet them if they come to the area for a recon trip. If you meet during their recon trip, they'll be rushed, because they are taking care of a lot of tasks in a short period of time.

The out-of-town prospects will understandably be nervous about trusting a stranger they have never met. They will need to feel they can trust you. One of the primary ways to build that trust is to do what you say you will do, when you say you will do it. If you are challenged in this area, don't work with the out-of-town prospect.

Another way to build their trust is to be as transparent as possible. Send them all documents that you will use so they know exactly what they are getting themselves into. These prospects will require patience. They are taking a big risk by trusting a stranger they have never met with their living space, one of the most important aspects of their lives. If you are not a patient person, don't work with this type of prospect.

Out-of-town prospects are usually temporary renters because they are moving into an area and want to take a little time to get to know it before permanently settling down. Require a minimum three-month commitment from the temporary prospect. The process of finding a tenant takes time and energy, plus you will likely experience loss of income due to vacancy time between tenants as an unavoidable part of the process, at least initially. It isn't worth it for less than a three-month commitment.

Credit Reports and Background Checks

Basics of Credit Reports

Credit reports are created from the information from three bureaus: Equifax, Trans-Union and Experian. Creditors, banks, landlords and companies who have been stiffed, medical providers, bad check reporting agencies and courts report credit information about people to these agencies, who in turn create a report about the individuals.

Bad checks, bankruptcies, foreclosures tax liens and judgments as well as information on credit accounts like credit cards, auto loans and mortgages are on the credit report. Besides credit information, credit reports contain other names a person may have used and addresses and employers over the years. The information is supposed to go back seven to ten years, but the bureaus frequently make mistakes, so information can go back longer.

From a credit report, you can create an idea about the prospect's debt load: Can he really afford the rent?

For room renting purposes, pulling from only one bureau is sufficient and less expensive. There might be information on one bureau that isn't on the other but most of the information is going to be the same. They are close enough for landlord purposes.

What to Look for on Credit Reports

Late payments and collections within the last 12 months
Bankruptcies and foreclosures within the last few years

Judgments
Tax Liens
Patterns of late payments
Old credit problems

You must have these specific items of information to pull a credit report:

- Tenant's full name (not nickname)
- Address
- Social Security Number or ITIN (Individual Taxpayer Identification Number for non-US citizens)

This information is requested on the longer version of the Tenant Application, along with their authorization allowing you to pull a credit report.

Basics of Background Checks

Background checks compile personal, financial, job and criminal information. They can search for information in a county, state and the entire U.S. They can verify histories for education, residences, marriages, divorces, court records, various other public records and criminal charges. You can use them as tools for looking into a potential tenant's past for previous incidents that may affect integrity and forewarn of potential problems.

It is possible to find background information through public records, internet searches and social media profiles. It is time consuming, but much of it is free or available for a small fee. You can save time by using a company that will perform the research relatively quickly for a fee. If you decide to use a company, it must be FCRA (Federal Credit Reporting Act) compliant.

When reviewing background information, consider patterns of behavior. One act is not the most efficient way for measuring a person's character. Look at consistent patterns of behavior, repeated mistakes and mishaps, not single incidents. People make mistakes. If given a chance, many people can reasonably explain a blemish on their records.

To Pull or Not To Pull

Pulling these, or saying you're going to, is an excellent screening tool. If you are concerned about being "cased" or allowing "undesirable elements" into your home, pulling a background check and/or credit report is the best protection.

Initially, I pulled credit reports; I have never pulled a background check.

Even when I found negative entries on a candidate's credit report, in the end it didn't matter. The ones who allowed me to pull a credit report and had credit issues usually had understandable explanations behind their troubles. If they passed my "radar" and other screening methods, I gave them a chance anyway. At one time when I had problems with my credit, plenty of people gave me another chance.

Ultimately, I decided that pulling credit reports was an unnecessary expense. But that's my experience and philosophy. I developed it over time with experience. You will develop your own.

I'm not as strict on a tenant's credit history as a landlord who is renting a separate rental unit. In my case, tenants are actually living with me. I see them on a regular basis. It's easier for me to bug them about the rent and harder for tenants to evade me because they are actually in my home. It's harder for them to sneak out without paying. It's also easier for me to evict them if they didn't pay their rent.

The Four Responses

As I mentioned earlier in Chapter 2, I developed a system that helps me screen applicants without pulling credit reports or background checks. I tell prospective tenants during the interview that I plan to pull a credit report and background check and ask them if there is anything they want to tell me about before I do. They have one of four reactions:

1. They immediately excuse themselves from consideration.
2. They tell me it's okay and then contact me later to tell me they're no longer interested.
3. They tell me about issues I would have found.
4. They have no worries because there's nothing to find.

Pitfalls of Screening Too Much

There is one problem with screening too much. If you go overboard, you can screen out too many people and lose too many good quality prospects. You'll have to find the happy medium between protecting yourself and risking the unknown.

One of the two poor tenant choices I have made was because I screened too much. It was early in my landlord experience; I was still nervous about the process, and therefore I was over screening. As a result, I ended up with too few candidates, and my vacancy period stretched too long, which strained my finances. I started feeling a little desperate, and I accepted a tenant I would not normally have taken. He was a mismatch from the start. He only lasted a month before he left by mutual agreement. We usually make poor choices when we're desperate.

The Legal Stuff

Per the Fair Housing Act and Fair Housing Amendments Act, you are allowed to pull credit reports on prospective tenants. If you decide to pull credit reports, you are required to pull them on all prospective tenants. Pulling credit reports on some applicants but not on others is considered discrimination. Also, you cannot set tougher credit standards for a member of any particular group (age group, ethnic group, sexual orientation, etc.).

The specific legalities vary from state to state. Do an internet search to confirm the rules for your specific state. Generally, you can charge a screening fee to an applicant, although the amount varies by state. If you charge for the reports, you are required to charge everyone and to give the candidate a copy.

You are required to get the prospective renter's permission before pulling his credit report. I include a few lines authorizing a credit report at the bottom of the long version of the Tenant Application form (see Appendix C). It says:

> By signing this application, applicant hereby authorizes landlord or landlord's representative to obtain and/or verify credit, employment, and rental history and information. Applicant who signs this application attests that the information provided in the application is true.

Since the information on a credit report is identity sensitive, it is essential to protect the information. If someone were to get a hold of the credit report, it could result in harmful identity theft. You would be civilly and financially liable, as you should be. NEVER leave a credit report, copy of tenant ID, tenant application or any tenant information out in the open, even lying around on your desk. The information must be kept hidden and protected in a filing cabinet or filing box. It is best to lock up this information. If you collect personal information from tenants, you have a responsibility to protect their privacy and identity.

Shred any private and/or identity sensitive tenant information that you no longer need. NEVER throw it away.

Where to Find Credit Reports and Background Checks

There are plenty of options for pulling credit reports on the internet. There are many companies on the internet that will pull credit reports for you; you just have to sign up with a credit-reporting agency and pay them. You can also employ tenant-screening companies, though they are usually oriented to landlords renting entire houses. Do an internet search. Try using "credit reports for landlords" as your search topic.

You can also do an internet search for background checks. Use "background checks for landlords" as a search topic.

When to Stop Looking for a Tenant

When do you stop looking for a tenant? When the cold hard cash is in your hot little hands.

Candidates will say they plan to take the room; they will ask for it to be held for them and then not follow through. Remember, room renters can be a flakey bunch. Require at least the deposit before you hold the room, and set a date for them to move in. Don't stop advertising and interviewing until you have at least the deposit in hand. If a desirable prospect knows that you're still looking, they will feel a sense of urgency to actually follow through and make a commitment.

Early on in my landlord experience, I interviewed what seemed to be a solid candidate for a tenant. He was enthusiastic about moving in. We made an appointment for him to return a few days later with the money and to sign the paperwork. I stopped running my ad and even turned away several prospects, and all the momentum for finding a tenant that I had built evaporated.

The appointment time came and went, but there was no tenant. I called his cell phone and he said he got caught at work but was on the major street leading to my subdivision as we spoke. Thirty minutes went by (more than enough time for him to arrive) but still he didn't show. I called his cell phone again; this time he didn't answer. He never showed and never called to cancel. Room renters can be flakey.

I learned from the experience to make sure that candidates understand I will stop looking for a tenant when the first person shows up with money in his hands. Several of my tenants moved quickly because they knew if they dragged their feet they were going to lose out. I have called a desirable candidate on several occasions to tell him another candidate was planning to come back the next day with cash in hand. If he wanted the room, he needed to show up before the other one with the money. When they're serious, they show up.

CHAPTER 6

THE PAPERWORK

Why?

This is a business venture for you. You need to create and maintain a professional manner to safeguard both yourself and your renter. To prevent misunderstandings, misinterpretations, hazy memories and potential legal issues, the rules and agreements need to be clearly expressed in writing. You will clearly express and explain those rules and agreements in the paperwork.

The paperwork is especially important if the parties are NOT strangers. If the landlord and renter are friends, family, work associates or acquaintances, it's essential to spell out ground rules and expectations. It can be easy for people who are familiar with each other to be too relaxed and negligent about respecting rules and boundaries. It can be difficult for landlords to hold firm with friends, family, work associates or acquaintances. There is more at stake with someone you know, such as the need to preserve existing relationships and maintain the dynamics of the shared social circle.

In keeping with a professional orientation, require prospects and tenants to complete and sign your paperwork.

Some people are going to be uncomfortable with the paperwork. These people are an unsuitable match for an organized, professional situation and have self-selected themselves out as candidates. If a person is uncomfortable with your professionalism, it indicates that they may be careless about expectations and boundaries and consider them tiresome and inconvenient. It's good to discover this before you have invested too much time.

The few times when candidates have become negative or critical, it has been when I introduced the professional paperwork. At this juncture they became defensive and inappropriate. When renting a house or apartment, applicants are required to complete a variety of legal, formal paperwork. It's an accepted and expected way of doing rental business.

Some candidates ask, "Why be so "formal?" It isn't formal. You are sending a message to candidates and the tenant that you are serious about doing things right and, though you may be friendly, there is still a professional component to the relationship. By setting boundaries from the outset, you are protecting both parties.

When candidates balk at the paperwork, you need to keep these points in mind:

1. Tenants will have access to your entire home.
2. Tenants will have access to and use of your personal property (furniture, appliances, kitchen items, etc.).
3. In case of emergency, you will need the tenants' emergency contact information to take care of them.

4. If tenants were renting a house or apartment, they would be required to complete an in-depth application, which they frequently have to pay for.

However, most prospective tenants are going to be comfortable with the professional orientation and paperwork requirement. They will be familiar with the process from their previous rental experiences, and your professional manner will promote reassurance about trusting a stranger with their living arrangement.

There is another important aspect to the paperwork for a landlord. If you have a tenant's personal information and the proper paperwork, it will be easier to collect money from the tenant, pursue protective or legal action, or even file a judgment, if ever necessary.

Protecting Private Information

Having candidates' or tenants' personal information requires care and responsibility. File or store it in a safe place. Never leave it casually lying around, waiting to be filed. Devise a filing/storage system and file the paperwork immediately. A locking cabinet is an excellent option for securing this personal information. Protect the tenant and protect yourself by immediately filing paperwork.

What Is This Paperwork?

There are four documents for every tenant to sign:

- Tenant Application (the long version or the short one);
- Month-to-Month Rental Agreement;

- Agreements Addendum (the rules of the house);
- Move Out Form (an excellent multi-purpose form).

These forms can be found in Appendix C.

Disclaimer: *I am not a legal expert and am not providing legal advice. Ultimately, you will need to do your own research for what is legal in your individual state.*

The Tenant Application

This is the first form in the series. There is a long version and a short version. The long version is two pages and requires the candidate to provide more information than the short one. It has a section where the candidate gives his permission for the landlord to pull a background check and/or credit report. The short version is one page, asks for less information about the applicant and doesn't contain the section granting permission to pull a background check or credit report.

Both versions require applicants to provide driver's license and social security numbers. This is the form with sensitive personal information that requires safeguarding. It's the only form containing personal identity information that, if stolen and misused, could wreak havoc on an applicant's life.

The long version asks questions about past negative experiences with landlords, delinquent rental experiences and foreclosures. If applicants have challenges in this area, this version will make them uncomfortable.

Eventually, I evolved to use only the short version. It's quicker and easier for applicants to complete. Most, even those who didn't have anything to hide, felt uncomfortable disclosing as much information as the longer version required. However, if you have a strong concern about letting in "undesirable elements," the longer version will screen them out.

Month-to-Month Rental Agreement
This legal document formalizes the verbal agreement between landlord and tenant. You can customize it for the amount of notice you require; amount of rent, deposit and money due at signing; whether pets, smoking or children are allowed; and anything else that is important to you.

I researched legal forms in books and on the internet; this one is specific to my state. You are welcome to use the one in the Appendix C but I make no legal guarantees or representations for it. Your best bet is to do your own research and tailor one to your specific needs and your state.

House Rules (aka Agreements Addendum)
This is essential! It is the key to being in charge.

Remember the difference between having a roommate and having a room renter is, "It's Your House, Your Rules." The House Rules or Agreements Addendum is the instrument that creates the control over your home and your life.

To retain influence and control over your living situation, you must present a written set of agreements or rules in an organized, professional manner. Without them you are stuck with tenants making their own choices, and you will lose control over your living situation.

The Agreements Addendum sets expectations between land-lord and tenant from the beginning. It spells out the living ar-rangement. It's the personal, social part of the contract between the two parties.

As you create these rules, think carefully about the living en-vironment you want. *You* decide what you want and what you will allow. Don't worry about getting it perfect in the beginning, because it will evolve over time. Just start with an outline, flesh it out and with time and experience, you can fill in the rest.

I have included my Agreements Addendum in Appendix C, which you can use as an outline. Use it to create your own. But first, a few cautionary words:

Don't go overboard, but don't wimp out. Creating the right set of Agreements enhances your competitive edge and creates a living environment that will work for you.

Initially, since I disliked the idea of sharing my home, I laid out strict rules. I also presented them at the wrong time. As a result my initial experience was unsatisfactory because I was scar-ing away prospects by being too strict.

Then I loosened up too much. When I presented the agree-ments to the tenants, I was tentative and down played their impor-tance. Because of my inadequate presentation, tenants tended to ignore the agreements, which in turn made me uncomfortable and annoyed with the tenants.

Over time, I developed a sense of what worked for me while still making my offering competitive. I found my confidence and presented my requirements accordingly. Over time you will too. Be patient with the process.

House Rules Versus Agreements Addendum

I found there was a subtle psychological difference between calling this form the "House Rules" or the "Agreements Addendum." I observed the difference in how tenants reacted when they were called House Rules and when they were called Agreements. I noticed that the term "Agreements" had a more positive impact. It also made a difference in how I presented them.

The term "House Rules" suggests a parental house with mom's and dad's rules. In contrast, the term "Agreements" creates a sense of adults agreeing on a system or set of policies. It's the same thing, but the different name creates a different reaction. In business, presentation and perception are important. If you want to inspire acceptance and compliance, it is important that you create a positive perception of the rules in the initial meeting.

When to Present Them

The old adage "timing is everything" is true in presenting the Agreements Addendum. I experimented with when to present them, and I found that presenting them at the wrong time scared away prospective tenants.

My mentor friend emailed prospective tenants her Agreements Addendum when they expressed interest in her listing, before she talked to them on the phone. When I did this, only a few responded again (and mine were less strict than hers). I found that emailing them at this point tended to scare away the prospects and made it more difficult to find a tenant.

Then I tried presenting the Agreements Addendum at the face-to-face interview. Some responded positively, some did not. Few expressed further interest in the room and I continued to have difficulty finding a suitable tenant.

Now I wait to present the actual written Agreements Addendum when the tenant comes to sign the Month-to-Month Rental Agreement; this has worked best for me. When I talk with prospective tenants during the face-to-face interviews, I have the Agreements Addendum in my hand and use it as my guide to discuss important issues and to ensure we are of a like mind. I clearly express my expectations during the interview and conduct an open conversation about lifestyle, habits and mutual expectations. Since we already thoroughly discussed the concepts during the interview, there are no surprises about my expectations. Nothing is being "sprung" on him. Both parties sign it and each keeps a copy.

Everyone Has Rules
Everyone has house rules or agreements. Most people don't think them through or put them in writing. Most landlords don't address house rules in any type of organized manner upfront, and the tenant figures them out the hard way, by bumping up against them as he makes mistakes.

One of my friends shared her daughter's room renting experience. A few months into her living situation, she learned she wasn't allowed to have sleepovers with male guests. She and her landlord hadn't discussed it in advance. When my friend's daughter brought home a male sleep-over guest, she ran into the landlord's unspoken rule, which created awkwardness and difficult feelings on both sides. It could easily have been avoided with honest communication upfront.

If necessary, the agreements can function as a tool to rein in a tenant. However, the likelihood that you will need that tool is significantly reduced because you have already expressed your expectations in writing. You have reviewed them with the tenant, he has signed it and you both have a copy.

One of my tenants frequently played video games with friends in his room. At one point, he and a friend were yelling at the top of their lungs for extended periods of time. This went on for several days. I kept thinking he knew better, and I expected it to stop. It didn't. I had a brief conversation with him about the noise level. He knew he should be quieter, because the noise level had been covered in the Agreements Addendum. He didn't argue and the yelling stopped immediately. Without the Agreements, it could easily have turned into a tug-a-war.

The Agreements Addendum also protected me when a tenant's girlfriend "unofficially" moved in. She was there nearly every day and night and her personal effects were multiplying in the bathroom. She was a sweet girl, but I didn't want two tenants. When I talked to the tenant about her being there too much, he argued. I pointed to the place in the Agreements Addendum where it spelled out the maximum amount of time a guest was allowed to stay over. His argument fizzled. Eventually we amicably agreed his housing needs had changed, and he moved on. Because of the Agreements Addendum, it was a friendly parting of ways.

Most importantly, by presenting the agreements early and in writing, you are taking responsibility for your expectations and exercising your choice to be in charge.

Contents of Your Agreements

You'll need to do some self-reflection to write Agreements that reflect your values, desires and tastes. Use my Agreements Addendum as a sample format. This form goes room by room, aspect by aspect.

Move Out Form

When a tenant gives notice that he will be moving out, immediately give him this form. It states how many days notice is being given, how much rent is due before the tenant moves out, and that the deposit will not cover the rent due. It also lists the cleaning tasks required before the tenant leaves. Signatures of both parties are required. This form makes it absolutely clear what the tenant is expected to do if he wants the full return of his deposit.

In my experience, tenants wait until the last minute to clean up and move out. If the deposit isn't sufficient, they will leave the cleaning to the landlord. Getting stuck cleaning up after tenants can delay your turnaround time. It takes time and energy to clean up the room, bathroom and other parts of the house to get it ready for the next tenant.

To speed up turnaround and save time and energy for more enjoyable aspects of life, charge a high enough deposit to motivate tenants to clean up after themselves.

There is more on this aspect in Chapter 8 – Nuts and Bolts.

CHAPTER 7

MANAGING THE RELATIONSHIP WITH THE TENANT

When the Tenant First Moves In

Many tenants will wait until the last minute to move in. Moving will be a simple process since most will bring few possessions. With this in mind, let the tenant know there will be a brief meeting when he first arrives to go over paperwork and collect the rest of the money. Set the expectation that he needs to make time for this initial meeting.

When he arrives, set the tone from the start. Have everything ready. The bedroom and bathroom should be clean. Clear adequate space in the refrigerator, cupboards, pantry and other spaces the tenant will share. Complete the paperwork and prepare anything else that is part of the offering.

When the tenant arrives, break the ice by having him inspect the premises. As you go through the house, show him the essentials: where the laundry detergent is, how the washing machine works, where the pots and pans are, and any other general or important information. Informally cover some of the information in the Agreements Addendum. Be friendly but professional. This is an opportunity to get to know each other a little better. This is the second first impression.

After the property inspection, go to the paperwork. This reinforces the impression that this is a professional arrangement. It doesn't have to take up a lot of time. It can take between 15 and 60 minutes, depending on how chatty you and the tenant are.

Go over the Month-to-Month Agreement to reinforce what the tenant has already verbally agreed to. Cover at least the following:

- The amount of rent, when it is due, when it is late, and cost of the late fee.
- Amount of rent (prorated for the first month if necessary) and deposit due at signing.
- The premises are in good working order and will be returned in the same condition as received.
- The number of days notice required before moving out.
- The utilities, water, cable, and internet are included.
- It refers to the Agreements Addendum several times.

At this point collect the money from the new tenant.

Next, go over the Agreements Addendum. During the interview, both parties have verbally agreed to the information in the form; the Agreements Addendum formalizes that agreement with signatures of both parties.

Next, go over the Application he completed at the interview to ensure all the information needed is on the form. Pay particular attention to the emergency contact information. It will rarely be needed but there will be times when it is.

It may seem counter-intuitive, but go over the Move Out form in this meeting. This spells out what the tenant has to do to get his deposit back and how many days notice is required. Some tenants are surprised at this form. They aren't expecting to talk about the end at the beginning.

Make sure you give the initial move-in meeting adequate time and attention. It's very important. Going through this process when the tenant first moves in sets the tone that you are in charge and this is a professional arrangement. Due to the flakey nature of room renters, many tenants may want to blow this off or take charge of it. Do not let them. This initial process is when you lay down the rules, which is crucial to building the landlord-tenant relationship.

Even if the tenant will only be in residence for a short time, this meeting is still crucial. My most disrespectful tenant was a short-term tenant. He was a person in transition. We both knew he was going to be there for three to four months. He tried to blow off the initial set-up meeting, and he bordered on derisive throughout it.

I was still relatively new at renting a room and was experiencing stretches of vacancy between tenants. Money was tight. I was in despair about filling the vacancy when he applied. Despite all this, I held my ground with the initial meeting and set the tone as best I could with this type of tenant. During his residence, he repeatedly pushed the boundaries, and I repeatedly pushed them back. At times he barely hid his disdain. If I hadn't held my ground with that first meeting he would have run all over me the entire three months he lived there. There are some tenants you will be glad to see go.

And lastly, make and give the tenant copies of everything he has signed. Assure him that you will safely file away the documents that contain his personal information.

All of these forms can be found in Appendix C.

Check-In Conversation after the First Month

I highly recommend a check-in conversation with the tenant after the first month. It doesn't have to be a meeting; your schedules will likely differ enough that a meeting won't be convenient. The conversation is usually brief and informal.

If you happen to be in the kitchen at the same time, or if you see the tenant on his way to/from the washing machine or some other casual interaction, start a conversation to see how things are going for him.

You can say, "I just thought I'd check in with you to see how things are going for you here. Is there anything you need? Anything that's not working very well for you? Anything I can do?"

It usually surprises and pleases the tenant you care enough to check in with him. If there is something he's uncomfortable with, you can deal with it early before it grows into something bigger down the road. This is the heart aspect of the "business arrangement with heart." You open the lines of communication by starting this conversation. It also helps keep the lines open if you check in again from time to time.

Communicating about Issues

As in any relationship, it's important to keep lines of communication open between landlord and tenant. If there are issues with behavior, muster the courage to talk to the tenant. Don't let resentment build until you set off a blast of pent-up negativity. If the tenant's behavior makes life easier, let him know. This is a business arrangement, but it has to have heart. It's your home, and it's the center of security for you and the tenant.

If discussing difficult matters is awkward for you, this experience will be your laboratory. It will teach you to speak up in a *respectful* way. The cards are already stacked in your favor because the house is your property. Remember that it is also the tenant's home.

If your schedules are quite different, it can be difficult to find time when you are both at the house (and awake) at the same time. It's acceptable to communicate casual information through notes if you set this expectation in advance. Setting this communication style in advance ensures that the tenant sees it as a respectful method of communication instead of a lazy or indifferent method.

You could write notes to tell the tenant that you need to enter the room for maintenance or repairs, the rent is due, the bathroom is dirty, or just to tell him thank you. It isn't ideal, but the alternative can be not communicating at all.

Don't use notes to communicate the tough topics. You have to muster good old-fashioned courage to communicate the tough things. Communicating tough topics with notes leaves too much open for misinterpretation and negative reaction.

Including Yard Work or Housework as Part of the Agreement

You may consider including yard work or housework as part of the rental agreement. My experience including them was consistently disappointing because I found that tenants didn't do the work they said they would. My mentor friend said she had the same experience.

I found that most tenants did not have the skills (or desire) to keep up their living environment. Few of my tenants had cleaned a bathroom before, and many didn't know how to sweep or mop a floor or mow a lawn. Having a home requires certain skills and commitment. People who rent a room in a home *tend* not to have either. If they did have them, they would probably be renting an apartment or a home of their own instead.

Collecting Rent

Rent (the extra money) is the whole reason you're renting a room in your house to a stranger. Depositing that extra money or paying off that bill makes it worth everything you've done to earn it. Wrinkles that delay you getting paid can range from annoying to financially crippling.

Designate a particular place for the tenant to leave the rent. It may seem like an innocuous detail, but it isn't. Your schedules will most likely be quite different and you won't see each other often. With a pre-arranged location, you eliminate delays or miscommunication about the rent.

Reinforce that the tenants must pay the rent on time. My experience was that most paid their rent on time. One renter regularly paid the evening of the fifth of the month, the last day before a

$10 per day penalty kicked in, but it was on time. If a tenant does pay after the fifth of the month, enforce the $10 per day penalty charge, as described in the Month-to-Month Agreement. Nothing communicates lessons more clearly than a thump to the wallet.

Do not relent for hard luck stories. Your boundaries are being pushed. If you give in here, there will be more. It's human nature.

One of my tenants told me he was having difficulties paying his rent by the fifth. He *told* me he was going to start paying the rent on the tenth. I reminded him of the late penalty clause in the Month-to-Month Agreement (which he had quite conveniently forgotten). I informed him it would cost him an extra $100 a month to pay on the tenth because the rent would then be ten days late at $10 per day. He was incredulous that I was going to charge him the late fee. I stood my ground and got the rent by the fifth every month thereafter.

If a tenant is successful at pushing boundaries in one place, he is most certainly going to push them in others. Relenting with one boundary makes it harder to hold firm against the next challenge.

On rare occasions I have split up the rent, allowing the tenant to pay half on the first and half on the 15th. Since I am essentially giving a two-week grace period for half the rent, I eliminate the five-day grace period.

A tenant that needs this type of long-term arrangement is going to be financially challenged. His income is small, or he manages his money poorly (or both). If you allow a five-day grace period for each half of the rent, the rent is likely to be paid late twice a month.

I caution against allowing this type of arrangement on a long-term basis. Allowing it for an occasional financial hardship is one thing, but it is not a good idea for the long haul. The tenant's financial challenges will create instability in his life, which will bleed over into the landlord's in one way or another.

If you decide to allow split rent payments, write it in the Month-to-Month Agreement and Agreements Addendum. Maintain strict adherence to the due dates.

Managing Noise Levels

If you are concerned about noise levels, cover this upfront in the initial interview. Set expectations at the beginning and reinforce them at the move-in meeting. By covering noise levels in the initial interview, you will screen out people without that social value.

On occasion, noise levels from the TV or a video game may rise beyond your comfort level. When this happens, just knock on the door and nicely ask him to turn it down a little. Don't wait until you're really irritated and hostile. Tell him sooner so that he gets accustomed to acceptable noise levels.

It may be your house, but you have to remember that this works both ways. Be aware of your noise levels. Are you banging around too early in the morning or too late at night? Is your music or TV too loud? If you're not sure what is disturbing to the tenant, ask. It shows you care about the tenant's comfort.

Taking Care of Your Responsibilities

Occasionally you will need to perform maintenance or repairs that affect the tenant. Good business dictates that landlords take care of responsibilities in a timely fashion. If you tend to be a procrastinator, don't procrastinate in this area. The tenant is paying to live in your home, so you must take care of your responsibilities that affect the tenant.

If the Tenant Doesn't Work Out

Most prospective rent-a-room-landlords express this concern. Many of the tenants are going to be short term. You can tolerate annoyances over the short term that you wouldn't tolerate over a longer term.

A tenant may be asked to leave for several reasons. Perhaps you made a poor choice. Or he was behaving resentfully for poor treatment.

Living with a tenant that you have asked to leave is uncomfortable and carries some risk. Retaliation is a possibility. Having a hostile relationship with a tenant disrupts both lives on a basic level.

No matter what, do not return this tenant's deposit until the full two-week time limit has nearly passed. This means you will also need the tenant's forwarding address. You need to allow enough time to find anything he's done or taken. Hold strong.

Trading Tenant Services for Rent

Rather than *including* tenant services as part of the agreement and rent, you may have the opportunity on occasion to *trade* tenant services for rent.

If you choose this option, be careful, you don't know the quality of the tenant's work. If you trade rent for handyman services, yard work or housework, deduct rent *only after* the work has been satisfactorily completed. Don't assume the tenant is going to do quality work. A tenant isn't going to have the same commitment to your house that you have. Also, he isn't going to have the same attitude toward the work as he would if he were actually getting paid money for it.

There are two keys to trading work for rent. One, communicate clearly what needs to be done and the quality of work expected. Two, give credit for the rent only after the work has been completed satisfactorily.

Trading services for rent doesn't necessarily mean you are going to get quality services for a bargain price. My kitchen faucet never worked quite right after a tenant installed it.

When It's Move Out Time

The moving out process can be the most delicate part of the room rental situation.

Moving is a stressful time for anyone, and people are not at their best when under stress. Frequently when a tenant is leaving, his vision is set on the horizon and not on what's in front of him. The need to get along with his landlord is diminished since he knows he's leaving. Some are challenged financially and will want their full deposit returned before they leave.

I don't want to give the impression that all tenants' departures are difficult or stressful. Most go smoothly. But you need to be prepared for the few that do not.

Protect yourself by making the move out process professional. Do not assume that you can relax because things have previously been friendly between you and the tenant.

When a tenant gives notice, *immediately* produce the Move Out Form. This form spells out what the tenant needs to do to receive the full deposit refund. It is dated and states the amount of notice being given (in number of days). It clearly states how much rent is due before the tenant moves, and that the deposit is NOT payment towards any remaining rent that is due. It also requires both parties' signatures. This form leaves no room for the tenant to misunderstand his responsibilities.

It isn't unusual for tenants to feel some level of discomfort with the formality of the Move Out Form. It effectively removes wiggle room for unique or creative interpretation of what they're supposed to do before moving.

You can present the form in a friendly, yet professional manner. Don't lose sight that this is a professional arrangement with a degree of risk. Your risk is greatest when the tenant is moving out. They have little to lose since they're leaving and most will likely never see or communicate with you again.

Don't hesitate. Be strong. Whip out that form. Renter/Roommate versus landlord/roommate disputes are some of the most common disputes on reality TV courtroom shows. The disputes are usually about how one party felt they got stuck by the other, because there was a lack of clarity and specificity between the parties.

30-Day Versus 15-Day Notice

I used to think a 30-day notice was required because that's how the process works with roommates or when renting an apartment or home. Surprisingly, I found it was more difficult when the notice was for 30 days.

There really isn't a need for a full 30-days notice. You don't need to prorate bills as in roommate arrangements, because all bills are included in the room renter scenario. The tenant doesn't have a lot of possessions to pack up. There is very little adjustment required on the landlord's part. The nature of the room renter arrangement is that it doesn't have a large impact on the landlord's life in the way a roommate scenario has.

Usually you can't show the room to prospective tenants while the current tenant is in residence, so even if you have more notice about the tenant leaving, you can't do anything about it yet. Their room and bathroom are frequently a mess and prospective tenants can't see beyond the reality confronting them. You are also invading the tenant's privacy when you're showing his personal space to strangers.

One note about the 15-day notice: If the tenant gives it before the 15th of the month, you will end up having to reimburse him for some of his unused rent. He will have paid a full month of rent on the first, but if he doesn't stay to the end of the month, he'll have overpaid his rent. As a result, I require the 15-day notice to be given *after* the 15th of the month so that I don't have to pay back any rent.

Don't Take It Personally

Remember, room renters are transitory by nature. My tenants are always surprised when I don't take it personally. I have heard many stories about previous landlords behaving badly and making life difficult once a tenant gave notice. Taking the tenant's departure personally only adds unnecessary stress.

Intervals between Tenants

Since you have to wait until the existing tenant moves out to show the room, you are going to have some vacancy between renters, which translates into some loss of income. How much depends on several things. It depends on how quickly you can turn the room around. It also depends on how prepared you are to start the tenant search process, how quickly you start it, and how diligent you are about it.

Turning the room around quickly will depend upon what condition the exiting tenant leaves the room and bathroom. If the room needs work after the tenant leaves, you have to invest time and energy to get it ready. How quickly you can turn the room depends on how busy your life is and how the room has been left.

Get ads prepared while the exiting tenant is still in residence. If you think the exiting tenant is going to leave his rented space in good condition, start placing ads on Craigslist a few days to a week before he moves out. It takes at least a few days before prospective tenants will be coming to the home to look it over. As you can see, "encouraging" the exiting tenant to leave his space "new tenant ready" is essential to quickly turning around the rental space and reducing vacancy time and loss of income.

Starting the Placement Procedure Again

Most tenants wait until the last minute to move out and clean up. You never know what condition they're going to leave the space in, or how much time it may take to get it move-in ready. Most often it will take some time and energy to clean up the room and get it ready for prospective tenants to visit.

Start placing ads during the week before the tenant moves out. It can take a week to build up momentum. Sometimes it can take two weeks if it's during the slower part of the month or season.

If you're left cleaning up after the tenant, finding time to fit it in can also create a delay. If you charge a high enough deposit and use the Move Out Form, the time you spend getting the room ready will shrink.

Most tenants are not going to take care of the space. Neglect creates some additional wear and tear on property. If the space is clean and repaired between each tenant, it mitigates the extent of wear and tear over time. It also creates a nicer looking, more competitive space to rent.

If the Key Isn't Returned

This is a common concern of would-be room-rental-landlords. It's never happened to me. I've had it left in the mailbox or under the front door mat, and the tenants neglected to tell me. When it has taken me past their move-out date to find the key, I deducted rent from their deposit for the days it took me to find it. Essentially, the room was not vacated or rent-able until I had the key in my possession. This is clearly stated in the Move Out form. It's also standard procedure for renting a house or apartment to return all keys when moving out.

If a tenant neglects to return the key, subtract the lock change fee from the deposit. This is another reason to wait to return the deposit.

CHAPTER 8

NUTS AND BOLTS

Deposit or No Deposit

A deposit protects the property. Remember, room renters tend to be flakey. They need to have some skin in the game and good reason to take better care of the property and leave it in decent to good condition when they move out.

Collecting a deposit perpetuates the professional tone. Deposits are required in a wide range of rental situations from apartments to homes to vacation rentals to equipment. They protect the landlord while communicating that the property is valuable. A deposit also ensures that the tenant feels a certain level of responsibility towards your home.

How much should you charge for a deposit? There are several factors to consider.

Since the tenant isn't using the entire house, the deposit doesn't need to be as large as if the entire premises are rented.

What will your market bear? Research Craigslist to see what the competitors are charging. Charge in the mid to higher end of the spectrum. Too big of a deposit can scare away prospects, but too little won't motivate departing tenants to leave the premises in an acceptable condition.

Figure out how long it will take to return the bedroom, bathroom and other parts of the house to good condition if they were left a complete mess. Figure out what your time is worth and multiply that by the amount of time estimated. This is just the foundation for finding your ideal security deposit amount; it will not be your final number.

I figured out how much my time was worth in conjunction with how much I dislike cleaning up after other people and put a price tag on it. It was $30 an hour and it took me four hours to prepare for the next tenant if the room was left a mess. I usually:

- Thoroughly vacuum and shampoo the carpet.
- Dust and polish the furniture.
- Wash off the shelves in the closet.
- Clean up the chair and other items in the room.
- Clean up the walls (room renters always do something to the walls).
- Clean the bedding. Wash and dry sheets, pillow cases, blankets, and mattress protector. Remake the bed.
- Thoroughly clean the bathroom. Sweep and mop the floor. Wash down the outside of the cabinets, the cabinet shelves and drawer interiors. Clean the mirrors. Scrub the counter tops. Polish the water and toothpaste-spotted fixtures. Scrub the bath tub and shower walls.
- Wash, fold and put away the towels.
- Remove trash and property items left behind.
- Clean tenant shelves in the refrigerator and throw away the old food items they left behind.

- Clean out the old food items left behind in the pantry.
- Clean up any messes they left in the kitchen.

More often than not tenants rarely if ever vacuum, dust, wash their sheets or clean the bathroom. Remember, most tenants don't have the skills and/or desire to keep up their environment. That's one reason they rent a room. When they do clean up before they leave, it will be done with varying degrees of skill or thoroughness. So far, after eight years of renting a room, there have only been two tenants who left things in a condition that warranted fully refunded deposits.

One of my departing tenants left a complete mess and told me he would pay a reasonable amount for me to clean it up. Don't let a tenant tell you what your time is worth. You decide and charge accordingly.

After calculating how much your time is worth to prepare the premises for the next renter, add an additional amount to cover repairs of possible damage to the property. I have settled on $200 for a deposit. It is in the higher range for my market. It covers me well if a tenant is irresponsible when he leaves. It's enough to scare away prospects who know they don't take care of the premises they rent. It's also enough to motivate most tenants to clean up at least most of the areas they've used.

When it comes to refunding the deposits, most tenants will pressure for its immediate return. Tough it out. Hold on to it for at least ten days. The law allows up to two weeks to return the deposit. Ten days gives you enough time to find damage that might have been done (and possibly hidden), a missed mess or missing property. If you put the returned deposit in the mail after ten days, the tenant should receive it within the 14-day window allowed by law. Be fair to yourself. Only refund as much of the deposit as the tenant has earned.

To receive the return of their deposits, tenants must provide forwarding addresses. This further protects you, the landlord, because you will know how to contact tenants after they leave if necessary. It also allows landlords to forward that inevitable mail that slips past tenants' forwarding requests. On several occasions W2s have come to my house after the tenants moved out, and I was able to forward them.

It's important to provide a thorough understanding up front of the requirements for the full return of the deposit. When they're leaving, tenants can get contentious over the deposit money when they want it back immediately. Sometimes finances are tight and they need the money for their next residence. Since they're leaving, they may not care about maintaining a cordial atmosphere. If you have made the details surrounding the deposit clear from the beginning, tensions will be eliminated or significantly reduced at the end.

Each state has different regulations regarding security deposits, time frames and conditions. Research the deposit regulations in your state before you set your requirements.

Prorating Rent

Fair business practice dictates prorating rent, so you only charge rent for the days the tenant is living in the home during the first and last months of residence. From my conversations with prospective tenants, many landlords do not prorate. Prorating rent makes landlords competitive, professional and sets them apart from the landlords who do not. It sets a tone of fair play from the beginning and continues it to the end of the relationship with the tenant.

Phones

Almost everyone has his or her own cell phone now. If there is a land line in your home, restrict tenant access to it. You can't control their usage, and you also eliminate the possibility of them not paying their share of the last bill.

Pets

Your Pets

Having pets is not an obstacle for room rental. It can be a screener for prospects who don't care for animals. However, many people will enjoy having pets around that they do not have to be responsible for. It's a kind of vicarious pet ownership for them.

Up to three cats and a dog have resided in my home (occasionally I'll foster another rescue dog) and it has not been a negative. Some renters have allowed my animals to hang out with them in the bedroom and loved them dearly. Some renters have been indifferent to them. People who don't like animals won't consider a home with pets.

Prospective renters and tenants are always concerned about noise levels, pet hair, pet odors and kitty litter odors. I've heard lots of stories about the smells and messes from previous landlords' animals. Having pets in the home requires staying on top of their noise levels, messes, hair and odors. I vacuum regularly, have a pet door to the outside and keep the kitty litter on the back porch. It's only fair to the tenants to provide a reasonably quiet, odor- and mess-free environment if they are paying good money to live there.

In the ad, include the fact pets are in the home, how many, and what type, so prospects will be forewarned. The non-animal-friendly ones will bypass the ad. Since so many prospects asked about hair, noise, messes, odors and behavior, I now include a few words about the pets in my ad. I include something like the following:

> I have 2 mellow cats and a small dog – all indoor/out-door and well behaved. There is no kitty litter indoors and no odor problem due to pet door. I keep the house regularly vacuumed and dusted so no pet hair.

In the Agreements Addendum, lay the ground rules for tenants regarding pets. Will the tenants be allowed to let them outside, take them for walks or feed them scraps? Any expectations either party has regarding pets should be discussed as early as the initial interview and then put in writing in the Agreements Addendum.

If animals exhibit behaviors a tenant will perceive as problematic, it will need to be addressed. Does the dog bark, jump on people or pee in the house? Do the cats sharpen their claws on things they shouldn't (like the tenant's belongings) or get into loud fights with one another? Do the birds screech early in the morning? Does the hamster run wildly on his squeaky exercise wheel at night? What type of environment will the animals create for a tenant who's paying to live there and wants a trouble-free living environment?

My dog barks at anything that goes by my living room window at night. If a tenant comes home after I've gone to bed, my dog will bark as if the poor tenant is a home invading ax murderer. He gets very protective at night. To shield my tenant from my dog's behavior, my dog sleeps in my bedroom at night. You will need to make concessions if your animals exhibit behavior that will create stress for a reasonable tenant.

Their Pets

When it comes to pets, people vary widely in their levels of responsibility and expectations for behavior as well as their abilities to manage their pets' behavior. What one person may consider indulgent, another may consider tolerating unacceptable behavior. What one person considers being strict, another may consider abuse.

Here are some questions to take into account if considering allowing tenants to bring their pets.

- If pets already live in the home, how well will they adapt to another animal in the house?
- How well will the home stand up to additional wear and tear a tenant's animal may add?
- How likely is the tenant to address damage from and behavioral issues of his pet?
- What behaviors will be tolerated from a tenant's pet?
- Will the pet be required to stay within the same confines as its owner? Or will it be allowed to wander more freely within the home?
- What will happen if you don't agree with a tenant's handling of his pet?
- What will cleanliness standards be for the tenant regarding his pet?
- What are expectations for the tenant to remedy issues created by his pet?

If pets are allowed, require an increased deposit. Imagine what type of damage may be done, how much it will cost to remedy and charge accordingly. Also, check with your insurance agent about how/if the extra animal will affect your homeowner's insurance policy. Some insurance companies won't write a policy if there are certain breeds living in a home; some will increase the premium.

Since I have cats and a dog and carpet throughout my house, I've adopted a "no pets" policy for my tenants.

Kids and Renters

Have Kids?
Households with children have another layer of responsibility to consider for both the family and the tenant.

There is the obvious concern about letting someone into your home who might harm your children. Smart phone apps and an internet search will quickly turn up a dozen options that will enable you to identify potential predators. You can perform background checks on any seriously considered candidate. You can also require references and check them. There are plenty of ways in the age of connectivity to protect families from potential wrong-doers.

On the other hand, a house with children is going to be a negative for many tenants. Background and reference checks, as necessary as they are, will be a drawback for many room renters.

Two of the things that tenants will be concerned about if children are in your home are noise levels and privacy invasion.

If a tenant is paying to live in your home, you have an obligation to provide an environment with reasonable noise levels and protected privacy. You will need to set and consistently reinforce boundaries for children's behavior.

In the Agreements Addendum, you will need to include many stipulations if there are children in the home:

- Ground rules regarding the tenant's interaction with children.
- Ground rules for the children regarding their interaction with the tenant.
- Guarantees to protect the tenant's privacy and peaceful living environment and how that will be accomplished.
- Elucidate how difficulties will be dealt with.

You will have to develop and add to these stipulations through trial and error. Having children in the home will require you to walk in both worlds, your family's and the tenant's, to maintain a successful experience for both parties.

Will Kids Be Allowed?

There will be some candidates looking for a room that allows children in one way or another. Some have custody of children who live with them full time. Some have shared custody, and the children live with them part time or every other weekend. Some have children or grand-children who visit for a few hours or occasionally spend the night.

The question will come up: Are kids allowed? If you allow tenants with children to live in your home, consider what ground rules will apply:

- Will they be old enough to understand the set boundaries and rules?
- How will the boundaries and rules be reinforced with the children?
- What ages will be allowed?
- Is the house kid-proofed?
- How will issues be dealt with that may arise if there is a serious disagreement about the tenant's parenting style?
- How much additional deposit will be required for the inevitable additional damage a child will create?
- How will you handle the special liabilities that come along with having children around who are not related to the landlord?
- If a child gets hurt in the home because s/he's just being a kid or not properly supervised, what type of liabilities are you prepared to risk?

Also, talk with your homeowner's insurance agent about how/if a tenant's children living in your home will affect your homeowner's insurance.

Respecting the Tenant's Space

When renting a house or apartment, the law requires the landlord provide 24 hours notice before entering the premises. Use this as a guide when it's necessary to enter a tenant's room. This is a professional arrangement. The processes described in this book are designed to set expectations for the tenant to respect your home and your rules. It is a case of reciprocal respect. You must respect the tenant's privacy.

Frequently when I've given the tenant 24 hours notice about entering his room, he told me I could enter whenever needed.

He made the choice. I showed the tenant the professional respect I expect.

There will be times when it is tempting to peek into the tenant's room when he's gone. Resist the temptation. It is an invasion of his privacy. Walk in the shoes of the tenant. How would it strike you if the tenant were peeking into the private areas of your home when you were gone? The tenant has one small area to call his own. It may be your house, but the tenant is paying to rent that space. Don't enter it without permission.

During my interviews with prospective tenants, I have heard many complaints of landlord privacy invasion. On many occasions it was given as the reason the prospect was looking for another place to live. It is frustrating for tenants to respect the landlord's boundaries but have their own ignored. It creates a sense of violation, lack of safety and disrespect. This small space is their home.

Another aspect of respecting the tenant's space includes staying out of the space designated for him in the refrigerator, pantry, cupboards, or wherever else he's being given space. The space he's renting is small, so don't encroach.

If you don't have enough room, purchase a used refrigerator or additional cabinet for the garage or porch. You can buy inexpensive self-assembly cabinets at home improvement stores or you can find low cost refrigerators at scratch-n-dent places.

A friend shared with me his frustrating experience with landlord encroachment. The bedroom and closet that he rented were filled with the landlord's possessions, and she frequently entered his room without notice or permission to access her belongings. She also regularly encroached on or completely took over the little room he was allowed in the refrigerator, cupboards and on bathroom shelves. A situation like this makes a tenant feel as if he's a paying guest.

Be Yourself - Neat or Messy

I was discussing the issue of being neat or messy and renting a room with a friend I was mentoring. She said she was a lax housekeeper so her house tended to be messy. Her tenants know up front it isn't going to be a neat and tidy environment. Her tenants know they can be relaxed about cleaning up after themselves. If they leave dishes in the sink for a few days, so what? If they don't clean their bathroom it doesn't matter to her. She attracts a type of tenant that doesn't care or want to worry about living in a neat and tidy house.

On the other hand, I'm fairly neat. I set expectations for tenants to clean up after themselves and not leave dirty dishes in the sink. My house in general is fairly neat and clean. Sometimes when prospective tenants come to the house for the face-to-face interview they express discomfort with such a clean place. On the other hand, it makes some feel more comfortable.

Whether you are messy or neat or somewhere in between, be yourself. Don't feel the need to loosen up if you're the neat and tidy type or tighten up if you're the messy type. Tenants come in a variety of dispositions with a variety of preferences. You'll attract the type of tenant that feels comfortable in the environment you provide.

Loosen Up - Tighten Up

At some point you may find yourself being too strict or setting your expectations too high. Conversely, you may find yourself not upholding your own guidelines and being too lenient, tolerating behavior or activities you're uncomfortable with. Especially in the beginning, it can be easy to be at either end, or both at the same time. It's understandable to initially be nervous about a stranger living in your home and how you're going to manage it. Eventually as you gain experience in the process, you will find a happy medium.

If you set overly high expectations for tenant behavior or expect guidelines or rules to be followed strictly at all times, it will create a tense environment of hyper vigilance. Tenants will feel like their privacy is being invaded and their lives are being micromanaged. Both you and the tenant will feel resentment, which leads to a tense, unfriendly atmosphere. These dynamics are byproducts that flow from fear of losing control at home.

For some, it can be difficult to set expectations and hold the line. If you fail to reinforce rules when there is an uncomfortable infringement, or if you tolerate boundary encroachments, you set up a cycle of continued infringement and encroachment. Your feelings of resentment and being uncomfortable in your own home will grow. This dynamic is created from fear of alienating the tenant and losing him.

Be patient. There are many variables to renting a room in your home. You will realize that it isn't just about the extra money, but also about creating a harmonious and peaceful living environment. Pay attention to the difficulties. Take responsibility for your contribution. This is your laboratory. You are experimenting. Learn from each experience.

The Past Is the Past

Occasionally you will have a difficult experience with a tenant. Human nature being what it is, it's inevitable. Don't hold past issues with former tenants against later ones. It's not fair to the tenant who hasn't earned your distrust or resentment. Let go of it. You are not fragile china. Resentment is like swallowing poison and expecting someone else to die. Stuff is going to happen and you'll survive it. You will learn from it.

The Taxman

I am not a tax expert, but I have prepared tax returns as a side business, and I was a tax consultant for a year and a half. The IRS requires you to report your rental income and allows you to deduct a variety of expenses on Schedule E.

The information in this section comes directly from the IRS's website, www.IRS.gov, and IRS Publications. In the search engine on www.IRS.gov, enter "rental income" and you'll find a large volume of information. You can also call the IRS at 800-828-1040 between early January and April 15 and talk to an IRS agent. I have condensed most of the pertinent information for renting a room in your home in the following section.

The information below assumes you are a cash basis taxpayer. This means you report income on your tax return for the year you receive it, regardless of when you earn it. Also, you deduct your rental expenses in the year you pay them, regardless of when they are incurred.

Reporting Rental Income

You will report your total rental income for the year on Line 3 of Schedule E, Part 1. After the expenses are subtracted, the total rental income or loss will be entered on the last line (Line 26) of this form. This amount is carried over to the first page of your 1040 form to Line 17. This amount in turn is added to or subtracted from your income, depending on if it is income or a loss. A nice characteristic of tax preparation software is that it puts the figures in the right places for you. You just have to input the numbers correctly.

Deposit

Do not include a security deposit as income if you plan to return it to your tenant at the end of the rental period. If it is used to cover the final rent payment, include it as income. If you keep part or all of the security deposit because your tenant doesn't live up to the terms of the agreement, include the amount you keep as income.

Services Traded for Rent

If the tenant trades his services for rent, you must include the fair market value of the services in your rental income. For example, if your renter performs plumbing services in trade for $200 deducted from his rent, you still have to report that $200 as rental income.

Expenses You Can Deduct

Expenses you can deduct:

- Advertising
- Auto and travel expenses – You can deduct the miles you drive if you pick up a tenant at the airport or pick up furniture for the room. You can even deduct miles if you make a trip to the home improvement store for a repair to the tenant's bathroom.

- Cleaning and maintenance – This includes housekeeping costs, yard care, extermination services and carpet cleaning.
  - o You can count all of the expenses for the room and bathroom you are renting.
  - o You can count a portion of the cleaning and maintenance costs for your home if you allow tenant privileges to use parts of your house.
- A portion of your homeowner's insurance
- Legal and professional fees incurred due to your room rental
- A portion of your mortgage interest
- Repairs (but not improvements)
  - o You can count the cost for all repairs for the room and bathroom you are renting.
  - o You can count a portion of the cost of repairs if you allow tenant privileges to use parts of your house.
- Supplies purchased for the tenant or rented room
- A portion of property taxes
- A portion of utilities (electricity, sewer, garbage pickup and water)
- Depreciation
- Costs to furnish and decorate the room
- Tenant's portion of internet and television service
- Dedicated phone line for the tenant
- Credit report and background check fees (for which you are not reimbursed by the applicants)

Proportional Share of Household Expenses
You can write off a proportional share of some expenses, like repairs, property taxes, utilities, depreciation, internet, television, and some other expenses.

To calculate how much of these expenses you can write off, calculate the size of the renter's bedroom in proportion to the rest of your house. Let's say the bedroom the renter uses is a 10-foot by 15-foot area. That's 150 square feet. Let's say your house is 1500 square feet. Divide the square feet of your home by the square feet of the renter's space (150 / 1500 = 10%). You can deduct ten percent of the repairs, mortgage interest, property taxes, homeowner's insurance, utilities, depreciation, internet, television, and possibly other expenses from your rental income.

Repairs Versus Improvements

You can deduct the cost of repairs (or a portion of them) but not the cost of improvements. A repair keeps your property in good operating condition and does not add value to the property. An improvement adds value to your property, extends its life, or adapts it for a new use.

Examples of repairs are painting, fixing leaks, and replacing broken windows. Examples of improvements are replacing or adding a fence or roof or replacing your windows with new energy-efficient ones.

Depreciation

You can also write off a proportional share of the depreciation of your property and cost of improvements from your rental income. This part gets a little complicated, so I won't cover the calculations here. It's best to use tax preparation software that can do these calculations or have a professional tax preparer do it for you.

If the depreciation for your property calculates to $5000 a year and you rent out 10% of your home, you can write off $500 as depreciation expense.

Keeping Records for Your Taxes

Chances are your tax return may never be selected for an audit. However, if it is selected, you'll need to back up all the income and expenses you claimed on your tax return with documentation. Keep this documentation for at least three years. If the IRS is really mad, they can go back as far as six years. I've seen it happen.

I suggest scanning all of your records each year and keeping an electronic copy of them. Some documents, like receipts printed from grocery stores or gas stations, fade over time until they are illegible. If the IRS can't read the receipt, you can't deduct the expense. I've seen that too.

To deduct a proportional share of the expenses mentioned above, you'll need to collect ALL those bills for the year. If you don't receive paper bills for some or all of them, make sure to download copies of the bills and keep them with the rest of your documentation.

To write off travel expenses, keep a travel log of the miles you drive as you go. Write down the location of where you go and record the round-trip miles. The IRS is concerned about "timely kept records." They want to see the records kept all along, not written up right before an audit. If your log is hand written and the handwriting is the same for the entire log, the IRS will disallow the expense. I've seen that too.

If the IRS disallows expenses, you may be subject to not only additional taxes but also penalties. Keep good records and keep electronic copies of them.

Helpful IRS Publications

There are IRS Publications that directly address rental income and expenses for your tax returns. Each tax year, the IRS Publications are revised to reflect each year's rules. Make sure to use the most current version.

- *Publication 527: Residential Rental Property*
- Section 9 of *Publication 17: Your Federal Income Tax*

What you do with this information is up to you...

CONCLUSION

Business Arrangement with Heart

This arrangement is about more than simply making extra money with another person living in your home. This is a reciprocal relationship. The tenant abides by the landlord's guidelines and pays to live in the home. He is responsible in co-creating a positive living environment. The landlord is responsible for providing a living environment that is healthy, sane and fair in exchange for those dollars and the tenant's agreement to live by agreed-upon guidelines.

Whatever you provide for a tenant goes beyond the dollars that are exchanged. A landlord has direct influence over the life of a tenant. The privilege of being in charge of your home comes with this responsibility.

Learn, Stretch, Grow

I continue to rent a room in my home, and I don't regret anything about my experience. The benefits have far outweighed the negatives. Initially I didn't want to have a stranger living in my home, but I had little alternative because of my finances at the time. The experience pushed me to operate way outside my comfort zone. I had to alter the way my home was set up and learn a wide range of new skills. To make it work, I had to learn from my mistakes. Over time I deepened my understanding of the dynamics between a landlord and a room renter, and I refined, refined, refined the process until it felt right. This endeavor can be an adventure that increases life skills and confidence.

I hope that this book will decrease your intimidation and increase your adventure.

Mentoring

If you feel you need a helping hand with becoming or being a landlord, I offer mentoring services. See my website at www. AntoniaMMartin.com for more information.

Appendices

Appendix A - Scams

There are a number of common and typical telltale signs in the scam emails. Below are a few typical examples pointing out the telltale signs. The scammer's purpose is to eventually get you to cash a bogus cashier's check and wire them money.

Craigslist has a webpage dedicated to education about scams. The following are excerpts from this webpage that specifically pertain to scam responses common to room rental ads.

- **DEAL LOCALLY WITH FOLKS YOU CAN MEET IN PERSON** - follow this one rule and avoid 99% of scam attempts.
- **NEVER WIRE FUNDS VIA WESTERN UNION, MONEYGRAM** or any other wire service - anyone who asks you to do so is likely a scammer.
- **FAKE CASHIER CHECKS & MONEY ORDERS ARE COMMON**, and **BANKS WILL CASH THEM AND THEN HOLD YOU RESPONSIBLE** when the fake is discovered weeks later.

Distant person **offers a genuine-looking (but fake)** *cashier's check*

- you receive an email (example below) offering to buy your item, or rent your apartment, sight unseen.
- cashier's check is offered for your sale item, as a deposit for an apartment, or for your services.
- value of cashier's check often far exceeds your item - scammer offers to "trust" you, and asks you to wire the balance via money transfer service
- banks will often cash these fake checks AND THEN HOLD YOU RESPONSIBLE WHEN THE CHECK FAILS TO CLEAR, including criminal prosecution in some cases!
- scam often involves a 3rd party (shipping agent, business associate owing buyer money, etc)

Thanks for your mail, Since the cost of your bike is $800 i just contacted my client about the cost of your bike and it present condition and he said there is no problem about that. So my client said he will be issuing you a Certified Check of $4000 while you wire 3000 to me through Western Union Money Trasfer and you deduct the cost of your bike $800 and keep the remaining $200 which my client said you should take for the terms of Transaction and Agreement between you and my client. So i will like you to send me your full contact information to where my client will be sending you
> the Certified Check like this:
> name.........
> full address.............
> city...............
> state.............

> country..........
> zipcode............
> cell/office/home phone number......................
> I will look forward to the requested information as soon as possible so that the check can be sent out to you immediately And do get back to me with the Pics of the bike so tha! t my client will be Able to see What he is paying off. Get back to me immediately. Looking torwards your respond,
> Best Regards.

Just insert a room rental situation in this response and it is a mimic of some that you will see. Usually the third-party allegedly sending the money will be portrayed as a male relative or work associate.

————

The first email from a scammer, however, *usually* does not start out offering to send money. The intention is to entice you into an email exchange where they will eventually request money to be wired back to them.

As in the Craigslist's example above, it will be obvious that English is not the writer's primary language. *This is not to say that everyone who isn't fluent in writing English is a scammer.* There are particular aspects to the writing that give away the email as a scam. If you would like to become more familiar with these specific aspects, read below. If not, skip to the next section.

Hi... my name is Shana. I'm 28yrs old. I would like to take the room. I googled the location and i like the environment. I like to move in ASAP, i'm clean and decent, respectful and i always pay my rents without any delay. tell me if a lady can move in. Thank you.

- Serious prospects do not introduce themselves the way this one does. "my name is Shana. I'm 28 yrs old." This is typical for scammers, as you will see in other examples.
- Most of the time they pose as young, seemingly innocent and sweet females. Sometimes they will even include sexy pictures of themselves.
- Most tell you they want to take the room ASAP without meeting you or seeing the room.
- There is uncommon word usage, such as she likes the "environment," she is "clean and decent, respectful," "rents" (rather than rent), "without any delay," "tell me if a lady can move in."
- They try to sell you on how wonderful, girl-next-door, they are. They invariably tell you they are clean, decent, respectful, etc.

———

From Sarah Bullock *(This one plays on the celebrity's name Sandra Bullock)*

Hello, *(Serious prospects never say Hi, Hello, etc. in an email. Small detail but it's another dead giveaway that you're about to read a scam email.)*

I am interested in your rental listing, i need a bed room Apartment space or a condo or a studio space any one of these available will be fine. Please provide me with the following informations; Is the unit you have available for rent now, Would I be responsible for paying the utilities?   will you sign a year lease? Do I need to pay any deposits? How secured is the area? Please, give me a reply to let me know if you will be of further assistance to me.

Thank you and God bless you

- Notice the wording and word usage is obviously by someone whose primary language is not English. (*Again, this is not to say that everyone who isn't fluent in writing English is a scammer.*)
- Punctuation, capitalization, word spacing, and spelling are frequently quite poor.
- They ask questions already in the ad, most likely because they are sending out mass emails to every email address in every posting, and they usually ask the same type of questions. Serious prospects don't usually ask these questions.
- They frequently say "bless you or God bless you." I've yet to see a serious prospect say that.

I am looking for some place in your area around the beginning of June, as I currently am in Italy and won't be back until mid-May, but I grew up in California and went to St. Mary's University for my undergrad. I am returning to do some post graduate studies while working. I am 25, social but responsible and respectful of those around me. I play soccer and am also active and enjoy being outside My only concern is that you have cats, I am allergic, are they in the house often? And if they are do they come into the other bedroom often? And I would love to see pictures if possible.

- It is very typical for scammers to say they are currently out of the country. Frequently they will claim to be from the US originally or to have lived here for some time.
- This one is selling herself as "social" (quite common), "responsible and respectful of those around me" (also quite common).
- If I had responded to this email as a serious inquiry, her next step would have been to tell me a male relative or close male associate would be mailing me a certified check or money order. It would be for too much money for some reason or another and she would want me to cash it, keep my money and wire the rest to her.

Room Needed, uRGENTLY
ROOM NEEDED ASAP!!!!!!!!!!!!!!!!!!!!!

- Again with the urgency, playing on your financial need.
- Incorrect letter capitalization and spacing.

Hi,

I consider myself a respectful, easy to get along, 59 years young, female. I am interested to have more information about the room you are renting, to see if it is what I am looking for. Thank you.

- Again with selling themselves, "respectful" and "easy to get along."
- Female, but this time she is older which is unusual.

- Incorrect or unusual word usage, "easy to get along" rather than get along with and "interested to have more information."
- Frequently use the term, "I am interested to have more information about the room."

Hello Roomie *(Very common for scammers to use the presumptive "Hello Roomie".)*

How are you doing? I saw your post on craiglist about the room so I decided to contact you to know if the room is still available because I`m so much in need of a room, and i`d like to know some details about the room and below are the questions i have for you;

1) Is the room still available?
2) How much is the totall house rent of the room?
3) What are the utility included?
4) Do you have any more picture of the room? if yes send to me

I shall be waiting for your swift response

- Serious prospects never ask "how are you doing" scammers frequently do.
- Word usage is that of someone not fluent in writing or using English.
- Again with the urgency.
- Asks a lot of questions that are already in the ad.

Hello,

How are you doing? I hope all is well. (*Typical scammer greeting*)

I'm sanyo rose, am 28 yrs old and Am originally from Barcelona, Spain. Graduate of Huelva University on the Costa de la Luz, I have a master degree in interior fashion and I work as a professional fashion designer.

Young female from out of the country. They seem to think the fashion industry is glamorous and sexy, so frequently the scammers have some association with fashion.

I moved to portland, OR four year ago for work and that's where am living befor i got a job in africa. I'm am not in the states right now, i am presently in West africa. I am work on contract for a company call (African Family Home Fashions) here in West Africa (Nigeria) which the contract has ended four months ago and i was hoping to see another job hear but i did not so i want to come back to the state..

- Claims to be living outside the US but has lived within and familiar with the US.
- Improper word usage, spelling and capitalization.

I will be returning to states lets say in two weeks time if i see a place that i will live cos i cont go to portland cos the house i was liveing has been sold out to another person. I enjoy traveling, It is very interesting to get more knowledge about the new countries, new

> people and traditions. It's great to have such a possibility. As i was searching through the web i saw the advert of your apartment and am okay iwth the prize you called it on the advert on craigslist ok so i will be happy rent from you ....

- It's common for the scammers to claim they like to travel and find out more about other countries.
- They frequently use the uncommon word for Americans, "advert."
- Willingness to rent without talking to you, finding out more or seeing the place.

> Now a little about myself;I am from Barcelona, Spain : that means i am Spanish and had all my education in Spain.

> I am currently living in africa now but my job is no more hear in africa so i want to move to the state and my mum is in spain who's a catholic volunteer worker, but also manages her antique business. She is a volunteer at the sister's of the eucharistic heart of jesus convent, there in Barcelona, Spain.. and am single, the only child of my only parent, my mother alive, i lost my father and my only brother years ago while i was still a kid in an auto accident..

> I have been wanted to relocated to the US longtime ago even while i was a little girl growing up and my mom is in support. It' been a long dreamed come true for me when i finnally settled in the portland, or US now.

I have chosen your city for me to live when i arrive. I am easy to get along with and well mannered. I do not use people's items without permission and consideration.. Kindly get back to me ASAP with the your monthly rent and the deposit i need to pay to enable you turn down other interested parties and keep the place for me until i arrive, because i will like to pay for the deposit before my arrival and i will like to know the total amount the rent for a whole year would be, as i am more interested in a long term lease, but still open to any form of lease you want.

- Too much personal information, a serious prospect would not share this type of information in a first email.
- Claims to be "easy to get along with and well mannered" and "do not use people's items without permission and consideration."
- Uses the term, "kindly get back to me" – very common for scammers, never used by serious prospects.
- Again with the urgency – ASAP.
- Asks questions already in the ad.
- Wants you to keep the place for her until she arrives – also common request.
- Wants to pay the deposit and entire rent for the year without any discussion.

But i will like to pay the deposit first of all before i arrive to show my seriousness and so that you can hold the place for me until i arrive. I am single as i said and i am not attached to anyone at the moment. I do part time modeling; i call myself an amateur though, LOL, just something i take as a hobby and also i have a masters degree in interior fashion which i bagged from the Huelva University on the Costa de la Luz in

Spain. I will be looking to pick up Fashion Designer jobs once i arrive in ur city, Fashion Designer is my life and i love it.

They frequently pose as a model to lead you to believe they are attractive, sexy and glamorous.

I am new living all alone as i have lived with my mom alone in the past but i have no doubs in my mind about my ability to live peacefully with as i was raised to be a lover of peace. A friend just introduced me to this thing and i really wish that i am able to find the good cultured kind of Place i am looking for here. I hope i am doing it right anyways. LOL.. Well, i think we will get along well because am a easy going person who respects ones privacy, like i said i dont do drugs or smoke but i drink only occasionally, i strongly believe there will be any problems living with me as i was raised by strong catholic Christain parents and have inbibed such good qualities from childhood.

I will love to see your pics and those of the place as well. I'll be so glad if you can reserve the room for me and remove all your the adverts abt the place as i'll love to rent the place. It will be nice if you could meet me online at my personal yahoo IM......sanyo_ rose2 or if you did not get me on line you can email on my hotmail..sanyo_rose2003@hotmail.com or sanyorose2003@gmail.com Get back to me ASAP

Thanks and have a gooday sanyo

Following are a few more typical scam emails. You'll be able to spot the scammer signs now.

> Hello there,
>
> My names are Amanda Wong by name, 25 years of age, Am from Richmond, BC. Very Gentle, I pocess a great Sense Of Humour, And i like Travelling to see new places most times. I respect people alot of which i expect in Returns,
>
> I will be relocating to the United States Of American {U.S.A}. Let me know your city again and states so as to be sure am mailing the right person.

> ———

> Hello,
>
> How are you doing? I'm interested in the room you have for rent. Kindly let me know the full details of the place.
>
> Hope to hear from you.

> ———

The purpose of this section is to familiarize you with the typical scams you're going to find. Unfortunately, you will see some of the same scam emails multiple times. If you familiarize yourself with them, you won't waste time and energy getting involved in an exchange, and you won't become a victim.

Appendix B - Ads

Sample Ads
Title: $475 Fully Furnished Room + Bills

$475 Fully Furnished Room For Rent Includes:

Large, light room with walk-in closet with lots of shelving;
The room is on the opposite side of the house from my bedroom
so it's like you have one side of the house to yourself;
High quality queen-size bed with bedding (you just need your
own pillows);
Large desk with large hutch, chair, table, TV, bedside table, ceil-
ing fan and other useful miscellaneous items (see photo album)
Shared use of screened in porch overlooking lovely back yard
and study/library for hanging out;
Utilities, cable, wireless internet (equivalent to $200);
Most housekeeping and all yard work; and Privileges for: kitchen
(fully equipped with everything you need – except your food),
dining room and laundry (I provide the detergents, etc.)
Best suited for temporary residents (3 to 6 months)

Large bathroom with ample cupboard space, towels and tub/ shower to yourself and just off the bedroom – very private.

Nice one-story, 1900 sq ft home in XXXXXX subdivision off *(major cross streets)* in safe, secluded, quiet, friendly, neighborhood with lots of trees - one block from green belt. Lots of parks, hiking, walking, as well as stores/shops and restaurants nearby. Bus stop is just a few blocks away. Also close to USAA, UTSA and Medical Center area. Quick access to *(the highway)*.

Looking for one quiet, person and no pets, drugs, or smoking; easy on the drinking or partying.

I have 3 mellow cats and a small dog – all indoor/outdoor and well behaved. There is no kitty litter indoors and no odor problem due to pet door. I keep the house regularly vacuumed and dusted so no pet hair.

I am a quiet, health, fitness and outdoor -oriented, single, business woman.

Photo album available. Month to month agreement is all required. Dollars for moving in are $475 rent (or prorated amount if moving in after the 1st) plus $200 deposit. Please respond to XXXXXXX@XX.com.

———

Title: $475 Furnished Room & Bills in Great House & Location

$475 Includes the Following:

Your own large, light bedroom with walk-in closet that has lots of shelving

The room is on the opposite side of the house from my bedroom so it's like you have one side of the house to yourself

High quality queen-size bed with bedding (you just need your own pillows)

Large desk with large hutch, chair, table, TV, bedside table, ceiling fan and other useful miscellaneous items (see photo album)

Large bathroom with ample cupboard space, towels and tub/shower to yourself which is just off the bedroom so there's plenty of privacy

All utilities, cable and wireless internet (equivalent to $200)

Privileges for: kitchen (fully equipped with everything you need – except your food), dining room and laundry (I provide the detergent, etc.)

Shared use of additional library/study and screened in porch that looks out into a lovely back yard for hanging out

Most housekeeping and all yard work

Best Suited For Temporary Resident of Three To Six Months Duration.

The house –
In a safe, secluded, quiet, friendly, heavily-treed neighborhood
Nice one-story, 1900 square foot home
Off *(major cross roads)* one block from a green belt quick access to *(the highway)*
Close to lots of parks, hiking, walking, as well as stores/shops and restaurants
Close to Medical Center area, UTSA and USAA
Bus stop is just a few blocks away

Looking for no –
Frequent partying
Drugs
Drequent drinking
Smoking
Pets

About me –
Business woman
Health, fitness and outdoor –oriented
Single and quiet

About the other furry residents –
3 mellow cats and a small dog (I walk him twice a day)
They are indoor/outdoor and well behaved so a renter without pets is a must
There is no odor or pet hair because there is a pet door to the outside and no kitty litter indoors
I regularly vacuum and dust so no pet hair

To move in –
$475 first month's rent (or prorated amount if moving in after the 1st)
$200 deposit
Your word you'll give me a minimum of 15 days notice when it comes time to move out (more is always better).

Please respond to XXXXXXX@XX.com. I will reply with an invitation to my Photo album. If you like what you see we can talk, you can visit the house, and/or I can email you the month to month agreement which is all that is required.

———

Title: $475 Furnished Room + Bills + Housekeeping

$475 Includes the Following:

Large, light bedroom with lots of light and walk-in closet with lots of shelving
The room is on the opposite side of the house from my bedroom so it's like you have one side of the house to yourself
All utilities, cable and wireless internet (equivalent to $200)
Large bathroom with ample cupboard space, towels with tub/shower to yourself which is close to the room for lots of privacy
Privileges for: kitchen (fully equipped with everything you need – except your food), dining room and laundry (I provide the detergents, etc.)
Most housekeeping and all yard work
Shared access to screened in porch that looks out into a lovely back yard and study/library for hanging out
High quality queen-size bed with bedding (you just need your own pillows)
Large desk with large hutch, chair, table, TV, bedside table, ceiling fan and other useful miscellaneous items (see photo album)

Best Suited for Temporary Residents of Three to Six Months Duration.

The house is in a safe, secluded, quiet, friendly, heavily-treed neighborhood, nice one-story, 1900 square foot home. It's off *(my cross streets)* one block from a green belt. Lots of parks, hiking, walking, as well as stores/shops and restaurants are nearby. Bus stop is just a few blocks away. Also close to Medical Center area, UTSA and USAA. Quick access to *(the highway)*.

Please no drugs, frequent drinking/partying, smoking, or pets.

Me – business woman; health, fitness and outdoor –oriented; single and quiet

Other residents - 3 mellow cats and a small dog (I walk him twice a day). They are indoor/outdoor and well behaved so a renter without pets is a must. There is no odor or pet hair because there is a pet door to the outside and no kitty litter indoors. I regularly vacuum and dust so no pet hair.

To move in - $475 first month's rent (or prorated amount if moving in after the 1st), $200 deposit, and your word you'll give me 15 days notice when it comes time to move out.

Please respond to XXXXXXX@XX.com. I will reply with an invitation to my Photo album. If you like what you see we can talk, you can visit the house, and/or I can email you the month-to-month agreement which is all that is required.

———

Title: $475 Fully Furnished Room and More

$475 Rent includes:
Large bedroom with lots of light and walk-in closet with lots of shelving
The room is on the opposite side of the house from my bedroom so it's like you have one side of the house to yourself
All utilities, cable and wireless internet (equivalent to $200)
Privileges for: kitchen (fully equipped with everything you need – except your food), dining room and laundry (I provide the detergents)
Most housekeeping and all yard work

Large bathroom, which is just off the bedroom for lots of privacy, has ample cupboard space, towels, tub/shower and is all to yourself

Shared access to screened in porch that looks out into a lovely back yard and study/library for hanging out

High quality queen-size bed with bedding (you just need your own pillows)

Large desk with large hutch, chair, table, TV, bedside table, ceiling fan and other useful miscellaneous items (see photo album)

Best Suited for Temporary residents of Three to Six Months Duration.

The house is a nice one-story, 1900 square foot home in a safe, secluded, quiet, friendly, heavily-treed neighborhood and one block from a greenbelt. Will send photo album upon response.

Close to Medical Center area, UTSA and USAA. Easy, 5 minute access to *(major cross roads)* yet neighborhood is nice and secluded. Close to lots of hiking, walking, biking parks as well as stores and shops.

I'm looking for quiet, drug free, nonsmoker who doesn't drink much and has no pets.

I am a quiet, fitness and outdoor -oriented, single, business woman.

I have 3 mellow cats and a small dog (I walk him twice a day) – all indoor/outdoor and well behaved so a renter without pets is a must. No odor or pet hair because there is a pet door to the outside and no kitty litter indoors. The house is regularly vacuumed and dusted so no pet hair.

To move in - $475 first month's rent (or prorated amount if moving in after the 1st), $200 deposit, and your word you'll give me at least 15 days notice when it comes time to move out

Please respond to XXXXXXX@XX.com. I will reply with an invitation to my photo album. If you like what you see we can talk, you can visit the house, and/or I can email you the month to month agreement which is all that is required.

———

Title: $475 Fully Furnished Room for Rent – Bills Included

$475 large, light fully furnished room for rent – with walk-in closet with lots of shelving. The room has a high quality queen-size bed with bedding (you just need your own pillows), a table, large desk with large hutch, a chair, TV, ceiling fan, bedside table and other miscellaneous useful items (see photo album). It's on the opposite side of the house from my bedroom so it's like you have that side of the house to yourself. All utilities, cable and wireless internet included (equivalent to $200). Use of large bathroom with ample cupboard/drawer space, towels and tub/shower is all to yourself and also just off the bedroom for lots of privacy. Comes with shared use of a nice library/ study and screened in porch for hanging out. Also includes privileges for laundry (I provide the detergents, etc.), dining room and kitchen (fully equipped with everything you need – except your food). I do most of the housekeeping and all the yard work.

Best Suited for Temporary Resident of Three to Six Months Duration.

House is one-story, 1900 sq ft in XXXXXX subdivision off *(major cross roads)* in safe, secluded, quiet, friendly, heavily-treed neighborhood one block from green belt. Close to Medical Center area, USAA and UTSA plus lots of parks, hiking, walking as well as stores/shops, restaurants and bus stops. Quick access to *(the highway)*.

Looking for one quiet, person with no pets because I have 3 mellow cats and a small (non-shedding) dog – all indoor/outdoor and well behaved. Don't worry about odor or pet hair because there is a pet door to the outside and NO kitty litter indoors. Also, I keep the house regularly vacuumed and dusted so NO pet hair. Please no drugs or smoking and easy on the partying and drinking.

I am a quiet, health, fitness and outdoor -oriented, single, business woman.

Month-to-month agreement is all that's required. First month rent (or prorated amount if moving in after the 1st) plus $200 deposit to move in.

Please respond to XXXXXXX@XX.com. Photo album available by request.

———

Title: $475 Furnished Room Plus Extras

$475 Fully Furnished Room in A Cozy, Homey House.

It includes -
Nice, light, good size room with walk-in closet with lots of shelving

The room is on the opposite side of the house from my bedroom so it's like you have one side of the house to yourself

High quality queen-size bed with bedding (you just need your own pillows)

Large desk with large hutch, chair, table, TV, bedside table, ceiling fan and other useful miscellaneous items (see photo album)

Large bathroom is all to yourself, has ample drawer/cupboard space, towels, tub/shower and is just off the bedroom so there's lots of privacy

All utilities, cable and wireless internet (equivalent to $200)

Most housekeeping and all yard work

Privileges for: kitchen (fully equipped with everything you need – except your food), dining room and laundry (I provide the detergents, etc.)

Shared access to screened in porch looking out into wooded area and library/study room for hanging out

Best Suited for Temporary Resident of Three to Six Months Duration.

The house is:

- A nice one-story, 1900 square foot home in XXXXXX subdivision off *(major cross roads)* down from the Wash Tub and Post Office on *(major street near my home)*.
- In a safe, secluded, quiet, friendly, heavily-treed neighborhood
- One block from a lovely green belt
- Close to lots of parks, hiking, walking as well as stores/shops and restaurants.
- A few blocks from a bus stop and lots of bus stops in the neighborhood

Near the Medical Center area, UTSA and USAA; Easy, 5-7 minute access to *(major cross roads)* yet neighborhood is nice and secluded.

Also, living at my home are 3 mellow cats and a small dog (walked two times a day) – all are indoor/outdoor and well behaved so a renter without pets is a must. No worries, there's no odor and no pet hair because there is a pet door to the outside and no kitty litter indoors. Plus, I keep the house vacuumed and dusted.

I'm looking for one person who is

- Quiet
- Drug and smoke free
- Easy on the drinking and partying

I am:

- Quiet and responsible
- Fitness and outdoor –oriented
- Single, business woman

Requirements to move in:

- 1ˢt month's rent - $475 (or prorated amount if moving in after the 1st)
- Deposit - $200
- Month-to-month rental agreement – signed

Please respond to XXXXXXX@XX.com. I will reply with an invitation to my photo album. If you like what you see we can talk.

―――――

Title: $475 Furnished Room in Great House & Great Location – Bills Included

$475 fully furnished, large room for rent with lots of light; walk-in closet that has lots of shelving; high quality queen-size bed with bedding (you just need your own pillows); a table, large desk with large hutch, a chair, TV, ceiling fan, bedside table and other useful miscellaneous items (see photo album). It's on the opposite side of the house from my room so it's like you have that side of the house to yourself. Includes all utilities, cable and wireless internet (equivalent to $200) as well as own bathroom. The large bathroom, which is all to yourself, has ample cupboard space, towels, tub shower and is just off the bedroom for plenty of privacy. Also includes shared access to study/library and screened-in porch that looks out into a lovely back yard for hanging out. There are privileges for: kitchen (fully equipped with everything you need – except your food), dining room and laundry (I provide the detergents, etc.). I do most of the housekeeping and all the yard work.

Best Suited for Temporary Resident of Two to Six Months Duration.

One-story house, 1900 sq ft in XXXXXXX subdivision off *(major cross roads)* in safe, secluded, quiet, friendly neighborhood with tons of old oaks one block from lovely green belt. Close to lots of parks, hiking, walking, mountain biking as well as stores/shops and restaurants. Lots of bus stops in the neighborhood too. Awesome location - close to UTSA, USAA and Medical Center Area. Quick access to *(the highway)*.

Would like one quiet, person without pets because I have 3 mellow cats and a small dog – all indoor/outdoor and well behaved. Don't worry about odor or pet hair because there is a pet door to the outside and NO kitty litter indoors. Also, I keep the house regularly vacuumed and dusted so NO pet hair.

Please no drugs or smoking and easy on the partying.

I am quiet, health, fitness and outdoor -oriented, single, and business woman.

Photo Album will be emailed upon inquiry. Month-to-month agreement with minimum 15-day notice (more would be better) is all required. Dollars for moving in are $475 rent (or prorated amount if moving in after the 1st) plus $200 deposit. Please respond to XXXXXXX@XX.com.

————

Title: $475 Fully Furnished Room Plus

$475 large room for rent with lots of light, walk-in closet with lots of shelving, a high quality queen-size bed with bedding (you just need your own pillows), a table, large desk with large hutch, a chair, TV, ceiling fan, bedside table, and other useful miscellaneous items (see pictures). It's on the opposite side of the house from my room so it's like you have that side of the house to yourself. Includes all utilities, cable and wireless internet (equivalent to $200) as well as own private bathroom. The large bathroom has ample cupboard space, own tub/shower, comes with towels and is just off the bedroom. Also includes shared access to study/library and screened-in porch that looks out into a lovely back yard for hanging out. There are privileges for: kitchen (fully equipped with everything you need – except your food), dining room and laundry (I provide the detergent, etc.). I do most of the housekeeping and all the yard work.

Best Suited for Temporary Residents of Two to Six Months Duration.

House is one-story, 1900 sq ft in XXXXXXX subdivision off *(major cross roads)* in safe, secluded, quiet, friendly, heavily-treed neighborhood one block from lovely green belt. Close to lots of parks, hiking, walking, mountain biking as well as restaurants and shops/stores. There are also lots of bus stops in the neighborhood. Only 10 minutes from UTSA, USAA, Medical Center Area and *(the highway)* access.

Looking for one quiet, person with no pets because I have 3 mellow cats and a small dog – all indoor/outdoor and well behaved. Don't worry about odor or pet hair because there is a pet door to the outside and NO kitty litter indoors. Also, I keep the house regularly vacuumed and dusted so NO pet hair.

Please no drugs or smoking and easy on the partying.

I am a quiet, health, fitness and outdoor -oriented, single, business woman.

First month rent (or prorated amount if moving in after the 1st) plus $200 deposit and month-to-month agreement with minimum 15-day notice (more would be better) is all that's required. Photo album will be emailed upon inquiry.

Please respond to XXXXXX@XX.com.

————

Title: $475 Furnished Room with Lots of Extras

$475 large fully furnished room in a cozy, homey house for one person with no pets

For $475, you get:
Nice, light, good size room with walk-in closet with lots of shelving
Bedroom is on opposite side of the house from my bedroom so it's like you have that side of the house to yourself
High quality queen-size bed with bedding (you just need your own pillows)
Large desk with large hutch, chair, table, TV, bedside table, ceiling fan and other useful miscellaneous items (see photo album)
Large bathroom with ample cupboard/drawer space, towels and tub/shower all to yourself and is just off the bedroom for plenty of privacy
Kitchen (fully equipped with everything you need – except your food), dining room and laundry privileges
Most housekeeping and all yard work
All utilities, cable and fast wireless internet (equivalent to $200)
Shared use of study/library and a screened in porch looking out into a lovely treed area for hanging out

Best Suited for Temporary Resident of Two to Six Months Duration.

The house is:

In a safe, secluded, quiet, friendly, heavily-treed neighborhood
One block from a lovely green belt
Close to lots of parks, hiking, walking, mountain biking as well as restaurants and shops/stores
A few blocks from bus stops
Within 10 minutes of UTSA, USAA, Medical Center are and *(the highway)*
A nice one-story, 1900 square foot home in XXXXXXX subdivision off *(major cross roads)* down from the Wash Tub and Post Office on *(major street near my home)*.

Other residents are 3 mellow cats and a small dog (I walk him twice a day) – all indoor/outdoor and well behaved so a renter without pets is a must. Don't worry, no odor and no pet hair because there is a pet door to the outside and NO kitty litter indoors. Also, I keep the house regularly vacuumed and dusted so NO pet hair.

If you are:
Quiet
Drug and smoke free
Low key on drinking
Please apply.

I am:
Quiet
Health, fitness and outdoor –oriented
Single, business woman.

Please respond to XXXXXXX@XX.com. I will reply with an invitation to my photo album. If you like what you see we can talk. First month rent (or prorated amount if moving in after the 1st) plus $200 deposit and month-to-month agreement with minimum 15-day notice (more is better) is all that's required.

Have a great week!

———

Title: $475 Furnished Room with Great Extras, Includes Bills

$475 includes:
Large, light semi-furnished room with large closet with lots of shelving
Room is on opposite side of the house from my bedroom so it's like you have that side of the house to yourself
High quality queen-size bed with bedding (you just need your own pillows)
Large desk with large hutch, chair, table, TV, bedside table, ceiling fan and other useful miscellaneous items (see photo album)
Utilities, cable, wireless internet (equivalent to $200)
Most housekeeping and all yard work
Privileges for: kitchen (fully equipped with everything you need – except your food), dining room and laundry (I provide the detergents, etc.)
Shared use of study/library and screened in porch that looks out into a lovely back yard for hanging out

Best Suited for Temporary Resident of Three to Six Months Duration.

Nice one-story, 1900 sq ft home in XXXXXX subdivision off *(major cross roads)* in safe, secluded, quiet, friendly, neighborhood with lots of trees - one block from green belt. Lots of parks, hiking, walking, hiking as well as shops/stores and restaurants nearby. Bus stops are very close. Only 10 minutes from UTSA, USAA, Medical Center Area and *(the highway)* access.

Looking for one quiet-ish, person with no pets, drugs, or smoking and easy on the drinking.

I have 3 mellow cats and a small dog – all indoor/outdoor and well behaved. There is no kitty litter indoors and no odor problem due to pet door. I keep the house regularly vacuumed and dusted so no pet hair.

I am a quiet, health, fitness and outdoor -oriented, single, business woman.

Photo album available. Month-to-month agreement is all required. Dollars for moving in are $475 rent (or prorated amount if moving in after the 1st) plus $200 deposit. Please respond to XXXXXXX@XX.com.

———

Title: $475 Furnished Room & Bills & Extras

The rent (for one person) of $475 includes:
Large, light room with large closet with lots of shelving
Room is on opposite side of the house from my bedroom so it's like you have that side of the house to yourself
High quality queen-size bed with bedding (you just need your own pillows)
Large desk with large hutch, chair, table, TV, bedside table, ceiling fan and other useful miscellaneous items (see photo album)
All utilities, cable and fast wireless internet (equivalent to $200)

Large bathroom with ample cupboard space, towels and tub/ shower all to yourself

Privileges for: kitchen (fully equipped with everything you need – except your food), dining room and laundry (I provide the detergents, etc.)

Most housekeeping and all yard work

Shared use of screened in porch that looks into a lovely back yard and study/library for hanging out in

The house - in a safe, secluded, quiet, friendly, heavily-treed neighborhood, nice one-story, 1900 square foot home. Only 10 minutes from Medical Center Area, UTSA, USAA and *(the highway)* access. Close to lots of parks for hiking, walking, biking as well as shops/ stores and restaurants and one block from a green belt.

Please no drugs, smoking, pets or frequent drinking and partying.

Me – business woman, fitness and outdoor –oriented; single and quiet.

Other residents - 3 mellow cats and a small dog (I walk him twice a day). They are indoor/outdoor and well behaved so a renter without pets is a must. There is no odor or pet hair because there is a pet door to the outside and no kitty litter indoors. I regularly vacuum and dusted so no pet hair.

To move in - First month's rent (or prorated amount if moving in after the 1st), $200 deposit, and your word you'll give me minimum 15-days notice (more is better) when it comes time to move out.

Please respond to XXXXXXX@XX.com. I will reply with an invitation to my Photo album. If you like what you see we can talk, you can visit the house, and/or I can email you the month to month agreement which is all that is required.

Template for Writing an Ad

Describe what is included in the room rental

Describe the bedroom and possibly its location within the home

Describe bedroom furnishings

Describe the bathroom (always important to renters)

Shared rooms or areas of your home

Identify privileges (like kitchen, laundry room, dining room)

Clarify if bills are included (which ones and how much they're worth)

Other amenities

If it's important to have a long-term or short-term renter, mention it.

Describe the strengths of your home and the surrounding area

One- or two-story and square footage of home

List major cross roads (optional if you want to list subdivision)

Features of the neighborhood (safe, secluded, near stores, parks)

List nearby points of interest (university, major employers, theme parks)

List access to major roads or highways

Accessibility to public transit, which is important to some renters

Other aspects that make it attractive

Briefly describe the type of person you are looking for:

Partier/No partying

Social/Quiet

Pets okay/No pets

Smoking okay/No smoking

One person, couple, kids okay
Other aspects

Briefly tell about yourself:
Single or married couple
Working person or retired
Male or female
A few other brief aspects

Tell about pets or children in the home:
Children – tell their ages and gender
Children – tell a little about them: well behaved, respectful of renter's privacy, busy with after school activities, gone every other weekend, etc.
Pets – quantity and types of animals
Pets – reassure prospects they are well behaved and the house is kept free of hair and odor (always a concern for renters)

Conclude by telling them about:
The photo album
Type of agreement
Cost of moving in
Your email address

Appendix C – The Paperwork

Tenant Applications

This is the first form in the series. There is a short version and a long version. The short version is one page, asks for less information about the application and doesn't contain the section granting permission to pull a background check or credit report. The long version is two pages and asks for more information about the client than the short one. It has a section where the candidate gives his permission for a background check and/or credit report to be pulled.

Short Version

Tenant Information

Name

_____

Date of Birth

_____

Driver's License Number and State of License

_____

Social Security Number

_____

Current Address

_____

_____

Length of time at that address

_____

Name, address and phone number of present landlord (if any)

_____

_____

Previous Address

_____

_____

Length of time at that address

_____

Name, address and phone number of previous landlord

_____

Name, address, phone number of emergency contact

_____

_____

Applicant who signs this application attests that the information provided in the application is true.

_____   _____
Applicant   Date

_____

Long Version

Tenant Application

Name

_____

Date of Birth

_____

Driver's License Number and State of License

_____

Social Security Number

_____

Current Address

_____

_____

Length of time at that address

_____

Name, address and phone number of present landlord

_____

_____

Previous Address

_____

_____

Length of time at that address

_____

Name, address and phone number of previous landlord

_____

_____

Names, addresses and phone numbers of any landlords in previous five years

_____

_____

_____

_____

Name, address, phone number, and name of contact person for applicant's employer

_____

_____

Name, address, and phone number of nearest living relative

_____

_____

Have you ever been evicted?

_____

Have you ever been in litigation with a landlord?

_____

If your answer to either of the above two questions is yes, please describe the circumstances. If any legal proceedings were filed, please list the count, state and case number of each of them.

_____

_____

_____

_____

Have you ever been convicted of a misdemeanor or felony?

_____

If yes, please explain

_____

_____

_____

By signing this application, applicant hereby authorizes landlord or landlord's representative to obtain and/or verify credit, employment, and rental history and information. Applicant who signs this application attests that the information provided in the application is true.

————————————————   ————————————————
            Applicant   Date

The Month-to-Month Rental Agreement

I researched books on legal forms and on the internet. It is specific to my state. You are welcome to use this one but I make no legal guarantees or representations for it. Your best bet is to do your own research and tailor one to your specific needs and your state.

Periodic Tenancy Lease

This lease agreement is made and entered into on *DATE* by and between *TENANT* (hereinafter referred to as "tenant") and *LANDLORD'S NAME* (hereinafter referred to as "landlord").

This lease shall create a periodic tenancy of one month, beginning on *DATE* and ending on the last day of that month. In the event that tenant makes the rental period for the month following the expiration of the periodic tenancy and is not in default of any of the provisions of this agreement, the lease shall be automatically renewed for the additional one-month period under the same terms and conditions as the original lease.

The leased premises are at *ADDRESS* and is for the exclusive use of *DESCRIBE WHAT TENANT WILL BE RENTING* (*i.e. of one bedroom; shared use of the library, screened in porch and a bathroom; and limited use of the kitchen, dining room and laundry*) as set forth in the "Agreements Addendum." There are no other tenants on these premises. (*If there are other tenants on the premises, list how many.*)

Tenant agrees to pay to landlord as rent for the leased premises the sum of *$HOW MUCH* per month, in advance, with the payments being due on the first day of each month beginning on *DATE*, and continuing on the first day of each month thereafter during the term of this lease. If the rent is not paid in full by the fifth day of the month in which it is due, tenant shall pay a late fee of $10 a day. Rental payments must be by check or money order. Cash payments will not be accepted.

In the event eviction proceedings have been instituted against tenant or a notice to vacate has been delivered to tenant, landlord may accept full or partial payments of unpaid rent. Acceptance of such payments does not waive landlord's right to proceed with eviction of tenant.

WHAT IS INCLUDED (*i.e. Utilities, cable and wireless cable*) are included in the rent as set forth in the "Agreements Addendum."

Landlord acknowledges the receipt of **$AMOUNT OF RENT COLLECTED** as the first month's rent under this lease as well as **$AMOUNT OF DEPOSIT** as a security deposit. In the event tenant terminates the lease prior to its expiration date, these amounts are nonrefundable. In addition, landlord reserves the right to seek additional damages if the damages suffered by landlord are in excess of the above amounts. In the event tenant defaults or is in breach of any of the terms of this lease, landlord may recover possession as provided by law and seek monetary damages.

Tenant stipulates that tenant has examined the leased premises and they are, as of the date of this lease, in good order and repair and in a safe and clean condition. Tenant agrees, at tenant's own cost and expense, to maintain the portion of leased premises mentioned above and as set forth in the "Agreements Addendum" in as good order, repair, and condition as they were in on the date of this lease.

TENANT SHALL REPAIR THE FOLLOWING, REGARDLESS OF COST, UNLESS CAUSED BY LANDLORD'S

NEGLIGENCE; WASTE WATER STOPPAGE CAUSED BY FOR-EIGN OR IMPROPER OBJECTS IN PLUMBING LINES, DAM-AGE TO DOORS AND WINDOWS, DAMAGE CAUSED BY DOORS AND WINDOWS BEING LEFT OPEN. TENANT SHALL GIVE LANDLORD WRITTEN NOTICE OF ANY CONDITION IN OR ON THE LEASED PREMISES TENANT BELIEVES AFF-FECTS TENANT'S HEALTH OR PHYSICAL SAFETY.

Tenant shall not make any alterations, changes or improvements to the leased premises without the written consent of the landlord. Any alterations, changes or improvements, other than moveable personal property, shall become the property of the landlord and remain on the leased premises after the termination of this lease unless the parties agree otherwise in writing.

Tenant shall not assign this lease or sublet the leased premises or any interest in the premises. An assignment or subletting by tenant in violation of this provision shall be void and shall, at the landlord's option, terminate this lease.

Landlord and landlord's agents have the right at all reasonable times to enter the leased portion of the premises for the purpose of inspecting them and for the purpose of showing the premises to prospective renters.

All notices or other communications required or permitted by this lease to be given to either party by the other party shall be in writing and shall be deemed served or delivered when personally delivered to the party or deposited in the US mail, postage paid, to the tenant at the tenant's last known mailing address and to the landlord at **LANDLORD'S ADDRESS**. Unless otherwise changed by written notice, all rent due and payable under this lease shall be paid to landlord at the above address.

(*Will pets be allowed?*) No pets of the tenant are allowed in or on the leased premises and as set forth in the "Agreements Addendum."

Should any litigation be commenced between the parties concerning the leased premises, this lease, or the rights and duties of either party in relation to the lease or the prevailing party's reasonable attorney's fees in addition to any other relief to which the prevailing party may be entitled.

If the tenant changes the locks or adds locks on the leased premises, tenant shall promptly deliver a copy of each key to the landlord.

The leased premises shall be occupied only by **NAME**. Guests are not allowed and as set forth in the "Agreements Addendum."

In the event tenant abandons the leased premises prior to the expiration of the lease term, landlord may re-let the premises and tenant shall be liable to landlord for any costs, lost rent, or damage to the leased premises. Landlord may dispose of any property abandoned by tenant and shall not be responsible to tenant for any such property.

At the expiration for the lease term, tenant shall immediately surrender the leased premises, in as good a condition as at the beginning of the lease term.

Tenant shall not use the leased premises for any illegal purpose or any purpose that will increase the rate of insurance or create a nuisance for landlord or any neighbors. Tenant shall not do any acts to harass landlord, other tenants, or neighbors.

Time is expressly declared to be of the essence in this agreement.

This lease shall be construed under and in accordance with the laws of the State of **YOUR STATE**, and all obligations of the parties created under this lease are performable in **YOUR COUNTY, YOUR STATE.** If any provision of this lease shall for any reason be held to be invalid, illegal, or unenforceable in any respect, the invalidity, illegality, or unenforceability shall not affect any other provisions of this lease and all provisions not declared invalid, illegal, or unenforceable shall remain in full force and effect.

The waiver by either party of any breach of any provisions of this lease shall not constitute a continuing waiver or waiver of any subsequent breach of the same or a different provision of its lease.

This lease contains the entire agreement between the parties and many not be modified except by written agreement which is signed by both parties. Any prior agreements or understandings between the parties, whether written or oral, are superseded by this lease.

TENANT GRANTS TO LANDLORD A CONTRACTU-AL LIEN ON ALL NONEXEMPT PROPERTERY IN, ON, OR ABOUT THE LEASED PREMISES. LANDLORD MAY SEIZE AND SELL SUCH PRPERTY TO SATISFY TENANT'S OBLICA-TIONS UNDER THIS LEASE BY PROCEEDING IN A CCOR-DANCE WITH CHAPTER 54 OF THE TEXAS PROPERTY CODE. LANDLORD IS ENTITLED TO COLLECT FROM THE PROCEEDS OF ANY SALE OR FROM TENANT THE COST

OF PACKING, REMOVING, AND STORING ANY PROPERTY SEIZED UNDER THIS PROVISION OF THE LEASE.

In witness whereof, the undersigned tenant and landlord execute this agreement as of the date set out above as the date of this lease.

_____   _____
Tenant, *NAME*   Landlord, *NAME*

The Agreements Addendum

Here is my form as an example. Customize to fit your needs. This is essential! It is the key to being in charge.

Agreements Addendum

Your Room - Please don't put tacks or nails in doors or closet doors or use tape of any kind on the walls, doors or closet doors (it pulls the paint off when removed). Eating in your room is okay as long as the carpet and bedding stay clean. Don't leave dirty dishes, food boxes, etc. in your room. If the carpet is made dirty or stained from food/drinks or the room smells of old food, you will need to remedy the problem by shampooing the carpets or whatever is necessary. Please vacuum the room at least once every two weeks to keep the carpet from getting trashed. If the door is open, the cats and dog will most likely enter.

Bathroom – Please keep in mind the bathroom you will be using will also occasionally be shared by my guests. So please keep it clean accordingly. Please use the fan when the room gets humid from the shower and leave the door open when not in use. This will keep the room from getting musty.

Kitchen – Please promptly wash your dishes and put them away or put them in the dishwasher. You may use the kitchen to cook your meals, please be respectful of kitchen appliances. Please keep your food/personal items in designated spaces. If you need more space at times, let's work it out. All items placed in the oven must have something under them, do not place items directly on the rack. If something you cook in the oven makes a mess in it, please clean it up. Do not place wet pots/pans on cook top, this ruins the ceramic. *Carefully* clean the cook top with designated light scrubber when necessary. When you use something, please put it back where you found it. Please don't place hot items directly on kitchen table or counter or leave food out on counters. Put your things away and wipe up your crumbs, spills etc. Please use a cutting board when cutting. The cats are not allowed on the counters. Feel free to use the squirt bottle provided to remove them from the counters.

Refrigerator - Please keep food in clean, sealed containers or bags, no open packages. Do not leave old food or dripping, dirty, leaking or spoiling items in refrigerator. Please keep your items in your designated space in the refrigerator.

Dining Room – You are welcome to use the dining room for your meals or hanging out. Please clean up after yourself. The cats are not allowed on the table. Feel free to use the squirt bottle provided to remove them from the table.

Living Room - is my personal space; however, you are welcome to use it when I'm not around. Please take your personal items with you.

Laundry room – is available for your use. Please do not leave your clothes (clean or dirty) in the laundry room or over stuff washer or dryer. Remove items when the cycle ends when possible. Clean lint filter after each use. Since I use "green" cleaners, use my detergent /bleach/softener at my expense. The last load can be put into the washer or dryer up until 8:00 pm and no earlier than by the time I am up in the morning. The laundry room is right off my bedroom and I can hear the racket the machines make. It tends to keep me up or wake me up when in use.

Library – is to be used as shared access with me. Except when otherwise arranged, please take your personal items with you. If you want to put your books in the bookcase I will gladly make room for them.

Screened in Porch – is to be used as shared access with me. Except when otherwise arranged, please take your personal items with you. No smoking allowed.

Front and Back Yards – can be used if noise level and behavior does not disturb me or the neighbors.

Property Use - Use of any other part of the premises, except those covered in this addendum, is not part of the rent and not allowed.

Trash/Recycle/Compost - I recycle/compost as much as possible and hope you will too. Please rinse off/out all recycle items before placing in recycle receptacles. Please do not put open food in trash that will cause odor and/or attract flies, take it directly to the trash outside if you're not going to recycle/compost. Use care in using the garbage disposal; make sure there are no unwanted items in it before turning it on; don't grind items that are too big or will create damage to the disposal. Most, but not all, food can be composted. Anything with meat, fish or dairy cannot be composted. Most unwanted bread or crackers can be given to the birds and squirrels. I will be responsible for trash, compost and recycle removal. Garbage that contains the odor of meat, fish or dairy will need to be disposed of in the outside garbage can since the cats and dog will tend to get into it if it's put in the kitchen trash can.

Cars and Parking - One vehicle is allowed plus an occasional guest's car. Car washing is allowed on the property. Auto maintenance may be allowed on the property with previous arrangement, including oil changes. There is safe parking on the street. Since the house is at the top of circle, very little traffic comes through.

Driving - Follow posted speed limits when driving through the neighborhood. Do not skid, peel out or drive aggressively through the neighborhood. Watch out for pets and children and be courteous to neighbors when driving, including no loud music that would disturb the neighbors.

Garage - is my personal storage space for my property and car. However, you can put your bike in the garage. Additional storage space in the garage may be negotiable.

My Pets – They come and go as they please through the pet door in the kitchen. Please do not feed scraps or treats to them. Don't take the dog anywhere without previous agreement or let him out of the front without being secured to the blue leash. If he is barking too much while leashed in front and disturbing the neighbors, please bring him in. Make sure the back gate is securely closed at all times. If you want to keep the animals out of your room, you'll need to keep the door closed. They love people and will probably want to hang out with you at times. You're welcome to squirt them with a water bottle to keep them out.

Other Pets – Animals, besides my own, are generally not allowed on the premises. If a guest is bringing a pet with him/her for a visit, this will probably be fine if the pet behaves itself. If the neighbors' dogs are disturbing you, please let me know.

Windows - The windows are all old retrofit double-pane and don't work very well. Please open and close with caution; you will likely have difficulty closing them again. If they are broken in the process of opening or closing, unfortunately you will be responsible for the cost of their replacement. The window in your bedroom has recently been replaced and can be opened and closed without any problems. For security purposes, please make sure it is closed and locked when you leave.

Doors and Locks - The front and back doors are to be kept locked at all times. Please don't let anyone you don't know enter my home or yard without prior agreement. Please don't slam doors.

Utilities, Cable, Internet, Phone, Mail – Electricity, gas, water, sewer, trash, cable and internet are included in your rent. There is no land line so you will need your own phone. Feel free to have your mail delivered to this address.

Utilities – In the summer I keep the house at 78-76 degrees between 6am and 10pm and 74-72 degrees between 10pm and 6am. In the winter I keep the house at 68-70 degrees between 6am and 10pm and 60 degrees between 10pm and 6am. If you would like to keep the house cooler in the summer or warmer in the winter, we can negotiate additional fees to cover the additional energy cost. Or you're welcome to use your own small room heater or fan. Please keep windows and exterior doors shut when AC or heat is on. Be mindful of saving resources: don't leave water running, turn off your lights, computer, fans, etc. when not in use or you're not around. Close your blinds when you leave during the day to reduce energy use.

Smoking – is not allowed on the premises.

Noise – Please keep down noise levels from phone conversations, television, music etc. Noise while in the front or back yards that would disturb me or the neighbors is not allowed. If my noise level is disturbing you, please let me know so we can negotiate what will be comfortable for the both of us.

Helping Around the House – Please just clean up after yourself and keep your personal items in your room or the bathroom and I will keep mine out of your way too. I will keep the house vacuumed and dusted to keep the pet hair to an absolute minimum.

Guests – Overnight guests of the renter are allowed up to three nights a week. Other guests are allowed as long as the place doesn't become grand central station.

Air fresheners - I am allergic to *some strong* air fresheners. We will have to get a feel for the air freshener if you prefer to use one.

Miscellaneous Behavior – Drunken behavior is not permitted. Drinking in the front of the house is not allowed. Drunk driving and illicit drug use is cause for eviction. If you break or ruin something, you are expected to cover the cost to replace or repair it. Please make sure your shoes are clean before entering the house. You are responsible for vacuuming/cleaning up what you track on the carpet.

Miscellaneous Other - Keep in mind, you are renting a room with shared access to various parts of the house and not renting the entire house. Owner is not responsible for lost or missing items.

My Office – This room is off limits.

Rent - Please pay your rent in full by the first of the month. If I am not home, you can leave the check on the kitchen counter. There will be a $10 a day charge for late payment. Non-payment of rent after the fifth of the month will be considered terms for eviction. A minimum of 15-days notice of intent to vacate is required, more is always better when possible, and must be provided AFTER the 15th of the month. Notice can be provided on any day of the month and needs to be provided via email or in writing as well as verbally.

Problems – Notify me immediately. If I am not on the premises call me at my cell phone at XXX-XXX-XXXX.

Questions - If you have questions about the house rules and/or would like to negotiate/discuss, please talk to me. This will be your home too and it needs to be a comfortable environment for both of us.

_____   _____
Tenant, *NAME*   Landlord, *NAME*

The Move Out Form

Here is my form as an example. Customize to fit your needs. When tenants give notice, this form is immediately given to them.

DATE

This is to acknowledge your notice to vacate the property as of **DATE**. It's been a pleasure having you in the house and I wish you luck and best wishes on your new adventure.

For the return of the full **$AMOUNT** deposit, the part of the premises that you've been renting needs to be returned in the same condition as received; therefore, the following is required:

- Leave the bathroom clean, including counter top, cupboard and drawer space, floor, tub, shower walls, toilet and mirror. Leave the faucet fixture clean and free of water spots. Empty the trash.
- Vacuum and shampoo carpet in your bedroom, closet and hallway leading to your bedroom. I will provide the carpet cleaner and carpet shampooer.
- Leave the shelves in the walk-in closet clean.
- Dust and polish the desk, its hutch and the table by the bed. I will provide the polish and dust cloth.
- Clean the table next to the desk and the blades of the ceiling fan.
- Cleanly spackle any holes in the walls of the bedroom that may have been made.
- Clean off any marks on the walls of the bedroom, closet and bathroom without damaging the paint. I will provide TSP to be used as the cleaning solution.
- Leave the room and mattress odor free.

- Leave the mattress and mattress cover in the same good condition as received.
- All sheets, pillow cases and towels freshly laundered and in the same good condition as received. *Please do not wash the comforter or decorative pillow covers.*
- Clean the shelves and drawer space in the refrigerator and shelves in the pantry that you used.
- Remove all personal property, including food in the refrigerator and pantry.
- Return the house key on the day you vacate the property.

Please keep in mind I have an aversion to cleaning up after people. If I have to clean up after you I will charge *$AMOUNT* an hour. Your deposit will be returned within 15 days so please remember to leave me a forwarding address.

NAME OF TENANT	*NAME OF LANDLORD*

ABOUT THE AUTHOR

A ntonia M. Martin has rented a room in her house for the last eight years. An analytical person who enjoys devising systems for just about anything, she created a turnkey system to make things easier.

Martin approached renting from an entrepreneurial business perspective based on fourteen years in the residential mortgage business. She has twenty-two years of experience in sales and marketing, extensive experience in training and mentoring, and has run two of her own full-time businesses and two of her own part-time businesses.

Martin's education includes a bachelor's degree in English and psychology and a master's degree in counseling. She lives in San Antonio, Texas, with two cats, a dog, and a tenant.